SANDRA ROSNER M.ED.

The Upward Bully in the Teaching Profession

How to stop your staff bullying the boss. A guide for school leaders and middle managers.

First published by SDR13 PTY LTD 2023

First edition

ISBN: 978-0-646-88402-8

Cover art by Tango Media
Editing by Jess Lomas

This book was professionally typeset on Reedsy.
Find out more at reedsy.com

Contents

Acknowledgement

In appreciation of Jim White, who suggested a book in preference to a PhD. To Sue Brown, Meghanne Wellard, John Baker and Dave Robson, the Directors of Educational Leadership who agreed to be interviewed for my M.Ed. To Sarah Branch and Michelle Barker, whose seminal research informed and guided me. Thank you both for your expertise and encouragement. To Sidney Dekker, who helped me find my author voice. To my beta readers, who patiently and thoroughly critiqued my drafts for ways to improve the message. John Fischetti, Jim White, Barbara Haddon, Judy and Bill Campbell, Toni Skewes, Andrew Turvey, Sue Brown, Robyn Stewart and Mike Mcnamara, I am indebted to you. My wonderful editor, Jess Lomas (and Reedsy.com, where I found her), as well as my fantastic cover designer, Ali Freile. Most importantly, to Dieter, who taught me that I should not only stand up for other people, but for myself as well.

Praise for this book

This book looks at an often-ignored issue within businesses and schools—the problem of the upward bully. The position of the principal in any school is a lonely one, where support based on a true understanding of the role can only be gained from colleagues at other schools. The role of a manager is to make decisions, and no matter how careful one is to negotiate and provide an inclusive environment in decision making, when the time comes to make that decision, there is always the chance that someone is not going to agree with the course of action being taken. Those who are not in agreement will then have the choice as to how they respond, and sometimes, fortunately not that often, this results in a series of actions that undermine the decision and the decision maker. As a result, upward bullying has commenced.

Within this book, Sandra has addressed this and suggested a range of strategies that can be taken to minimise the impact of this type of behaviour. This book is full of useful strategies for those facing upward bullying and is one to have on the shelf ready to consult when or if required. However, its greatest strength comes from its clear discussion of the impact and the suggested strategies, and I would highly recommend it to anyone stepping into any management role. This book allows new (and existing) managers to be prepared and able to identify upward bullying before it impacts their ability to lead and manage with a clear head and in a non-emotional state so that decisions can continue to be made rationally, allowing the decision maker to survive for the long-term and continue their work improving student outcomes.

Andrew Turvey (M.Ed.)
Deputy President NSW Secondary Principals Council 2015–2021
NSW Secondary Principal 2011–2021
CEO Together4Youth 2021–present

Aristophanes warned that you can't teach a crab to walk straight; luckily for education leaders, not all bullies are crabs. Sandra Rosner offers practical advice to help manage the manageable—the rest are probably sociopaths!

Judy Campbell
Head Teacher, Teaching and Learning, Barraba Central (K–12) School

Every school leader is all too familiar with dealing with students who exhibit bullying behaviours. And they are unfortunately often familiar with staff-on-staff bullying. In this thoughtful and practical guide, Sandra reveals the behaviours bullying staff are exhibiting toward their bosses. Upward bullying is a growing trend, and Sandra's experiences and advice are welcome and timely in a post-COVID world where so many colleagues are not well and taking it out on those above. You'll be glad you read this and learned from her examples.

Professor John Fischetti
Pro Vice-Chancellor The University of Newcastle, Australia
Past President, New South Wales Council of Deans of Education

This is a 'must read' book for anyone considering working in an executive position in school systems worldwide. *The Upward Bully in the Teaching Profession: How to stop your staff bullying the boss*, provides essential information to help understand bullying in the workplace and the potential impact on the individual. Included are a number of approaches to overcoming situations in leadership where the leader is being undermined.

The clever use of hypothetical situations allows the reader to relate to the trauma that is associated with bullying. Sandra Rosner has used her extensive experience in educational leadership to identify potential problems and provide effective solutions to help school executives deal with bullying in the workplace in a proactive way. This book should be helpful to all educators as it provides insight into human behaviour in the workplace and strategies for creating a highly effective leadership team in challenging environments.

Dr James White, PSM,
Manager of Schools and University Connect
Regional Director of Education in NSW (Ret.)
Fellow of the Australian Council for Educational Leaders

Sandra Rosner calls out toxic and Machiavellian bullies in schools. Safe schools start with safe leaders.

Bill Campbell
Professional Officer, NSW Secondary Principals' Council Inc.
Past Principal Peel High School, Tamworth, NSW, Australia

As an educational leader myself, Sandra's insight into upward bullying resonated with my own experiences in schools over 35 years. Her case studies are realistic, and her advice is wise and measured. I would recommend this book to any leader, regardless of their career stage. Upward bullying is unacceptable in schools, and leaders must be empowered to address it in a constructive manner. Sandra tells us how this can be done.

Sue Brown
Director, Educational Leadership, Mid Coast Valleys, NSW, Australia

Finally, a well-researched book presenting a range of details that address a major issue faced increasingly by executives, and especially principals, in all education systems. Reading this text acknowledges in a clear and conversational manner the many ways bullying unfolds and allows personal reflection and a clear path to discussing the matter in the open

Toni Skewes
Principal Ashford Central (K–12) School, NSW, Australia

Sandra Rosner is a very experienced educator and school leader. Sandra has drawn on her own experience and her extensive research to write an engaging and instructive handbook for school leaders. The use of case studies and practical hints and tips is of particular value.

Michael McNamara
Executive Officer NSW Secondary Deputy Principals Association.
Past Deputy Principal Murwillumbah High School, NSW, Australia.

International terms

In the book, I primarily use Australian terminology. Here, you'll find explanations of common educational terms and titles used in different parts of the world.

The head of a school:

- Principal (Australia, USA, Canada)
- Headteacher/Headmaster (UK)

Other executives:

- Deputy Principal/Assistant Principal/Vice Principal (Australia, USA, UK)
- Head Teacher/Head of Department/Dean (e.g., English, Mathematics)

The first year of school:

- Kindergarten (Australia, USA, Canada)
- Reception (UK)

The organisation where parents, teachers and school staff work together:

- Parents' Association/Parents and Citizens Association (P&C) (Australia)
- Parent-Teacher Association (PTA) or Parent-Teacher Organization (PTO) (USA) Canada, UK)

Teachers federations or organisations:

- Teachers federation (Australia, Canada) [federation members/representative]
- Teachers unions (USA, UK) [union members/representative]

Preface

Do what I say. Don't do what I do.

If schools across the world were to receive a report card on how we manage adult bullying in our workplace, I believe that F for Fail would not be uncommon. In a profession where we collectively put a great deal of sustained effort into teaching children the curriculum and how to be collaborative, collegial and kind to each other, adults working in schools have a poor reputation for leading by example.

The most inexperienced of classroom teachers soon learns how to mediate conflicts between children and among families, being tough on the problem and considerate of all parties involved. We quickly learn to achieve positive outcomes in our dedication to shaping the development of future respectful and respectable citizens. Teaching and support staff overwhelmingly agree that bullying is detrimental to student learning and wellbeing and should not be tolerated in classrooms or playgrounds. Child and adolescent bullies and mobs, bystanders and targets—whether actual or potential—are recognised and taught by us so that schools are bully-free zones, but only in relation to our students.

While disengaged or troubled students can be challenging, and a growing proportion of their parents and carers can be tricky to work with, these two groups combined have historically attracted much less angst for us as school leaders than problem staff have. This is evidenced by Professor Phillip Riley's longitudinal survey, The Australian Principal Occupational Health, Safety and Wellbeing Survey (IPPE Report).

Bullying of adults by adults in schools is a problem that is not sufficiently understood, acknowledged or addressed, regardless of our geographic and political circumstances. Workplace bullying in general—and adult bullying in schools in particular—has not yet attracted the attention it warrants, considering the damage it causes to individuals, families, workplaces, local community, society and the economy. While many researchers, companies, agencies and governments around the globe have been turning their minds to bullying in the workplace across the last 30 years or so, the attention afforded has been sporadic at best, and the take up by those in a position to make the greatest impact for the better has not yet hit its tipping point.

Without sufficient recognition or acknowledgement of the problem, a systemic approach to managing adult bullies in schools has not been set in place by organisational leaders in any country, state or province. This is despite the abundance of longitudinal data provided by injury notifications, hazard reports and complaints that are clear evidence of the widespread deleterious effects of upward bullies. Strategic methods of dealing with people who bully their bosses in organisations and businesses have been researched and documented. Theoretical and self-help books have been written on the subject. However, this research and these books do not currently apply specifically to the educational environment of our primary and secondary schools. In writing *The Upward Bully in the Teaching Profession,* I aim to highlight the human and contextual factors that promote upward bullying. I further hope that the information and the scenarios presented will enable principals[1] and other school leaders to confidently manage adult bullies in their workplace.

As a young teacher, I put in early and sustained effort towards achieving my professional aspirations. I have held positions ranging from head of faculty to deputy principal and principal in several schools in two jurisdictions. I have worked in large suburban high schools, very small remote schools, distance education schools and schools that cater for children from Kindergarten[2] through to young adults, with special education facilities for multi-categorical disabilities units attached. I have been an adviser to school staff, principals and directors of schools concerning equity programs, effective teaching and learning methodology and the theory and practice of school leadership and management. In short, I have worked in a broad range of educational settings. In every one, I have witnessed and experienced workplace bullying in all three of its manifestations: downward, horizontal and upward. Of these three types of negative adult behaviours, I have found upward bullying to be the least understood and, in my opinion, the most damaging, simply because when leaders are undermined, the adverse effect on the entire school community is disproportionately destructive. A damaged leader gives rise to a dysfunctional workplace.

The more I recognised, understood and dealt with upward bullying, the better I became at managing it. Over time, I gained a reputation for my ability to minimise the impact of adult bullies in schools. Principal and executive colleagues sought my guidance and acted on my advice, gaining confidence and, most importantly for me, passing on what they learned from the process to others. Over time, informed by my own experiences and those of my colleagues, I developed a suite of strategies that work in managing a range of upward bullying scenarios.

[1] Headteacher/Headmaster (UK)

[2] Reception (UK)

Introduction

The problem of upward bullying in the teaching profession is a complex one. It's difficult to identify or analyse and, consequently, to address or solve. The big problem is that the multifaceted and often hidden nature of upward bullying makes it challenging to identify every piece of the puzzle we must consider when dealing with adult bullies in our workplace.

Upward bullying is not a common term but is a common practice— albeit largely unrecognised and misinterpreted. The term 'bullying' in its current manifestation is a relatively recent one and, until even more recently, has only been applied to the actions of children and young people. In the 1970s, in northern Europe, schoolyard bullies attracted the attention of academics. Research on this phenomenon subsequently trickled through education departments in Europe, Canada, the USA and Australia over the ensuing years. By the turn of the century, we began to see a growing interest in the understanding and management of adult bullies. In the last couple of decades, an increasing number of researchers have contributed to identifying the occupations most often affected by a bullying culture. These occupations, counterintuitively, include many of the helping vocations; police, nurses, paramedics and teachers are overrepresented as occupations suffering upward bullies in their work environments.

As bullying has become a more compelling topic for researchers of adult behaviour, the primary area of interest has been downward bullying, in which the boss bullies their workers. This is a much more easily identifiable and measurable form of bullying than horizontal (peer-to-peer) or upward bullying, attracting more acknowledgement and support. Most departments of education would have established structures and strategies to support worker complaints against school leaders who bully them. Processes are well established in these departments to investigate bullies holding formal positions of power in schools.

Of greater concern, there has been a lack of exploration into the impact of upward bullying on the school leader, students and the wider school community. Upward bullying is the most suppressed form of adult bullying for various reasons, which I will explore in the coming chapters. Firstly, I'd like to explore some human and contextual aspects contributing to upward bullying in teaching.

Human factors

When school leaders are not given the support they need to deal with upward bullies, they are left vulnerable to attack from staff members who disregard authority and are allowed or enabled to become more emboldened over time. Upward bullies are naturally confident, self-obsessed and have an inflated sense of self-entitlement. They will push back when challenged unless their practices are exposed and negated. All leaders are potential targets as age and experience have less of a role to play than you might imagine. Even the most emotionally intelligent leaders will find themselves challenged by upward bullies who will make attempts on anyone; how their target reacts determines the bully's next moves. When faced with workplace bullies, the behaviours we turn to hold the keys to our success or failure in standing up to and minimising the impact of those who dare to bully the boss.

The Upward Bully in the Teaching Profession will help you identify and recognise traits of upward bullies and those we, the targets of their attention, possess. It will guide you to examine, review and learn how we might act and react, refining our interactions to diminish negative outcomes for ourselves, colleagues and students. It will sift through the human factors at play and the contextual enablers of upward bullies on our staff that compound the difficulty of our ability to deal expediently with them. After all, any competent principal can manage similar behaviours in members of the parent community. The context in which staff members feel emboldened or enabled to bully their bosses adds a layer of complexity to bullying behaviours beyond those exhibited by families and carers who target school leaders.

Contextual factors

The social behaviours and norms of our workplace directly influence how staff behave towards each other and their supervisors. Formal leadership alone does not set workplace culture; informal, non-positional leadership is a recognised aspect of the school leadership dynamic. However, unsurprisingly, adult bullies thrive in dysfunctional workplace cultures. Sometimes, they are merely opportunists exploiting the weaknesses of the school leadership.

A toxic work environment can give rise to the emergence of upward bullying behaviours. Elements of a toxic environment can include but are not limited to inadequate training, unrealistic expectations and insufficient resources. Where a school community is in a state of prolonged stress, upward bullies are likely to emerge. Where staff capacity is called into question, perhaps in a formal investigation of performance or conduct, upward bullies will push back in a concerted attempt to remove attention from their behaviours and to place the blame onto 'the person in charge'.

The relationship between human and contextual factors that enable upward bullying to thrive is likely bi-directional, and in an established poor work environment, it is difficult and probably inconsequential to delve into which came first.

Change management

Further complexity is added to the mix when those above impose system-wide changes. School leaders are expected to implement the changes and be accountable for how well the change processes are managed, as well as for the quality of the resulting outcomes. The influence of the upward bully is likely to gain traction when school leaders negotiate the way forward through such periods of change management.

When managing change, two factors can challenge a school leader in addressing emerging or existing bullying behaviours. The first of these is resistance to change. If staff do not fully understand the changes that they are expected to enact, nor have effective ways of implementing the changes, when they feel unsure or unsupported, they will resist those changes (in ways that we school leaders cannot, no matter how much we might like to). In such a climate of resistance, the upward bully will more easily gather support for insurrection.That support will be both active, in the form of mobbing, and passive, whereby bystanders observe, ignore and therefore appear to tacitly endorse the bullying of the targeted leader. The ego-driven, self-seeking bully skilfully exploits this dynamic. We'll examine mobbing and bystanding in later chapters.

The second factor to consider when negotiating change is the capacity of the school leadership team to steward the process effectively. Whether the change is system-wide or school-based, school leaders—first and foremost, the principal—need to have the leadership capacity to effect real change by steering their team through it. If a school leader is unable or unwilling, unconvincing or ineffective in managing change, they become an easier target for the activities of upward bullies. When the extent, volume and rapidity of changes are unrelenting, this will further destabilise their ability as leaders to settle the team before the next onslaught of demands for ongoing change is upon them. The sense of being overwhelmed and constant change fosters an environment that allows a bully to gain traction.

Significantly, the more practice you get at managing upward bullies, the less they will be able to impact you, your staff and the students in your care. Of course, until the debilitating effects of bullying behaviour aimed at school leaders are recognised, acknowledged and managed at a systemic level, progress across the board will likely remain sporadic and ineffective. In the meantime, as principals and school leaders, we can develop strategic methods to get on the front foot in dealing with upward bullies in our profession, looking out for ourselves and each other on a case-by-case basis until our respective systems catch up.

How this book can help you

Each chapter of this book is designed to impart information about a particular aspect of upward bullying, advance your understanding of the complexity of the concept and the experience, and provide advice for dealing with staff who bully the boss.

Each authentic scenario is compiled from real-life situations and tells a story of how a target has been bullied, how they reacted and the outcome. As you move through the scenarios, you might think you recognise a particular person in one or more cases; however, each scenario is a composite, and I don't reference an actual person in any situation. They may feel real to you because the actions are common to adult bullies in schools.

In the first chapter, we will delve into the three recognised types of workplace bullying to help you understand why upward bullying has gained less recognition than it deserves. I will clarify the concept of upward bullying in our workplace in Chapter 2 to enable you to determine if you are a target of upward bullying by one or more of your staff members, whether they be teaching or support staff.

Chapter 3 acknowledges the current lack of knowledge, understanding and support around upward bullying and exposes the myths around the practice. Similarly, in Chapter 4, we will unveil what is known about the nature of the two distinct types of upward bullies and expose some myths about their motivations.

Examining the nature of the target in Chapter 5, I reveal that contrary to expectation, they are not necessarily less experienced or less capable leaders and managers.

Chapters 6 and 7 examine the roles of the mob and the bystander, highlighting the interconnectedness between bullies, targets and their social environment. Chapter 8 takes a closer look at the environmental factors that support the existence and growth of upward bullying within the teaching profession.

Addressing the impact of change management in the rise of upward bullies, Chapter 9 emphasises how rapid, multifaceted or poorly managed changes can create fertile ground for the rise of upward bullies.

Lastly, Chapter 10 evaluates the existing systemic supports for managing upward bullies and preserving your wellbeing, while also discussing potential future directions for departmental policies and procedures surrounding upward bullying in the teaching profession.

1

Three types of adult bullies

It is reasonable to expect that sometimes every one of us operates as our worst selves. We might be worn down, overcommitted or distracted, causing us to be intolerant, demanding or short-tempered. In and of itself, this doesn't make us workplace bullies. Bullies are motivated by the need for power and influence; their poor behaviours are habitual and ongoing; they cause psychological harm, are self-justified and entitled, and lack empathy for their targets. They ignore the wellbeing and basic rights of those around them. Of course, some school principals, deputies and heads of faculty definitely fit that description. These leaders can be accurately labelled as downward bullies.

Downward bullying

Downward bullying is the most often reported and researched form of adult bullying, and some school principals are as guilty of this as any other workplace leader. Downward bullying is easy to visualise and empathise with. After all, who hasn't, at some point in our careers, suffered a narcissistic or even sociopathic school leader who enjoyed stomping around and shouting down their hapless staff members to gain compliance through fear? Or perhaps you've endured a lazy supervisor who has manipulated others to carry their workload and then brazenly taken the credit, as evidenced by their highly embellished applications for promotion.

At face value, downward bullying seems to be the most widespread of the three types of bullies we encounter in teaching. It is an entrenched cultural feature in some schools, set by the principal, then duplicated by deputies and middle management towards teachers, teachers towards their students, and older students to younger ones in a downward spiral of incivility. This situation denotes an unhealthy school culture wherein the rights and wellbeing of others are ignored.

It is, however, easy to blame the boss even when they do not deserve it. School leaders who foster good workplace relations, embed effective support structures and promote role clarity and sound organisational change management processes might nonetheless find themselves the target of upward bullies. Instructional leadership can be misconstrued by disgruntled workers to avoid doing the work that is expected of a proficient teacher. Because downward bullying is often self-reported, some teachers with a vested interest in maintaining poor customs and substandard practices can quickly identify themselves as victims of downward bullying. This occurs when things aren't going as they would like—when they are simply being asked to do their job more efficiently, behave collegially, effect workplace changes, or learn new skills commensurate with the direction the department dictates from above. Bosses who reasonably expect and encourage professional conduct and a positive work ethic from every staff member are at risk of being seen in the same light as authentic downward bullies.

Lateral or horizontal bullying

Where formal power is equal, there is still the opportunity for teachers or executive members of staff to use informal power to bully each other. You might be familiar with meetings, discussion groups or professional workshops where one or two of your peer school leaders have imposed their will on their colleagues through force of personality, loudness of voice or frequency of comment. Similarly, your own executive meetings can reveal much about your middle management when you take the time to observe how they relate to each other around the table: who runs the agenda, who distracts or opposes, who sits in silence and what each of them takes back to their faculties—not just the information from the executive meetings but how they deliver it.

Take note of who sits in the prime seats or takes up the most space in the staff common rooms, who dictates the topics of conversation and how often, and how many staff members regularly sit together at break times. From this, you will gain a good understanding of who creates the culture in the room and who has the informal power. Informal power is not in itself a bad thing—it's a feature of every workplace—but if it is gained and maintained via intense and frequent aggression, your school has a problem. When the informal power holders behave in a way that causes harm to their colleagues, this becomes a psycho-social hazard and is not just distasteful but illegal.

Lateral bullying is less recognised than downward; it can be more subtle to detect, and targets may not wish to indicate that colleagues on their level have gained power over them, as it can be seen as an admission of an inability to stand their ground. Lateral bullies gain traction when their peers avoid confrontation and thereby accept the behaviour of the bullies.

Targets of upward bullying can be even more reticent to admit to being bullied by their own staff members.

Upward bullying

Leaders and managers don't often report upward bullying, so it's difficult to accurately measure how widespread the practice is (see Rosner, S. *Upward Bullying in the Workplace: a literature review*). Academic studies indicate that somewhere between one in 10 and one in three workplace leaders are subjected to upward bullying behaviours. These figures alone indicate the need for more data. The teaching profession (along with nurses and police) has a higher incidence of upward bullying than other professions. Philip Riley's longitudinal *Principal Occupational Health and Wellbeing Survey* of school leaders in Australia, Ireland and New Zealand provides rich data collected over a 10-year period about the stresses of the principal's job.

It evidences emotional demands, burnout and depressive symptoms much higher than in the general population. Principals consistently identified offensive workplace behaviour as a major source of stress and reported adult-to-adult bullying at over four times the rate found in the general population. The recurrent recommendation for urgent systemic support arising from Riley's work has not yet been forthcoming, which is cause for concern in terms of work health and safety legislation. In the meantime, we can better prepare for and deal with adult bullies in our schools by learning from the experiences of others.

In Case Study #1, we meet Tony, who has several concerning encounters with Susan, a new member of his executive team.

Case Study #1: Lashing out in all directions

Tony was cautiously hopeful after the phone call from Human Resources. He had not been able to secure a permanent head of English at his rural high school over the last three years. Now, it seemed that HR had found a highly experienced and well-qualified head teacher. She was a country girl at heart and so knew the advantages and the drawbacks of working in a small conservative country town. She'd come with a glowing reference from her previous position and sounded lovely on the phone. Tony could hardly believe his luck.

Susan had been at the school for less than a week when she requested a formal meeting with Tony to 'clarify her position'. She brought a support person from outside of the town with her. Tony was not too concerned about the meeting. He got on well with Deidre, the district counsellor, and looked forward to catching up with her at Susan's meeting. He liked to see his middle managers take initiative and was not as prepared as he should have been, given this rather obvious red flag.

When Susan arrived bearing armfuls of documents, Tony began to experience a sense of unease. Susan came out firing.

'I've asked for this meeting with you, Tony, because you're in charge of those dreadful people in the student wellbeing team.'

Tony was taken aback to have Susan attacking some of his best staff. 'Could you tell me more about what you mean by "dreadful"?'

'They're horrible, all of them.' Susan was already hyperventilating, 'They don't treat the children with respect'.

'I'm really surprised to hear that. Could you give me an example?' Tony was scrambling to get his head around the implications. There must have been a misunderstanding.

'That young fellow, Darren. The one you've put in charge of wellbeing. He ridiculed poor James from Year 9. James said he wanted to play professional football, be a fullback. Darren made a joke about it at the meeting, and

5

EVERYONE laughed. It was so disrespectful. I can't possibly work with him. I can't work with any of them.'

'But Susan,' said Tony, trying not to smile, 'James has made that joke himself. You've seen him. He's 16 years old and weighs 40kg soaking wet. He'd never make a fullback. And Darren is not only a peer head teacher, he's also on your staff, teaching junior English. You have to be able to work with him, both as his colleague and as his faculty leader. We have to sort this misunderstanding out.'

Susan wasn't impressed. She clearly thought that Tony was not taking her complaint seriously. She insisted that Darren be disciplined for his disrespect and removed from her staff. Tony countered that she had the wrong impression of Darren, and after some tears and further accusations, Susan agreed to a meeting with Darren to clear the air. Susan went on to examine the intricate details of the job she was required to do. She complained that Tony had not inducted her sufficiently, provided an adequate office, or treated her with respect as a professional. The meeting dragged on.

Afterwards, Deidre was apologetic. Neither she nor Tony had seen this coming. They had both entered the meeting with goodwill to ensure Susan was settling in well. Deidre could see that Susan was attempting to use her as a lever to put pressure on Tony and was not about to play that game. A meeting to clear the air with Darren was obviously the way forward.

But the meeting never happened. Somehow, Susan was always unavailable to meet with Darren. But every week, she hit Tony with a new complaint about her faculty staff or peers. Eventually, she started in on Tony's deputy, then Tony himself.

Susan ultimately complained about the stress of being bullied by Tony and other members of staff to her doctor, who signed off week after week of stress-related sick leave. While on leave, Susan wrote lengthy letters to the school director, the president of the parents' association[1] and even the education minister, complaining about Tony's misogynistic treatment of her. Tony received a formal 'please explain' letter from his director. He was obliged to spend hours compiling documentary evidence justifying his position and detailing Susan's unprofessional behaviours. Meanwhile, Susan sat tight at home on paid sick leave, firing off vitriolic letters in all directions. Tony was obliged to defend himself and Darren repeatedly against increasingly malicious accusations. At the same time, the school still had to function without a permanent head of English and with an increasingly worn-down principal and despondent English faculty.

Tony ran into Susan's previous principal at a network meeting.

'Barry, that glowing reference you gave for Susan, what was that all about?'

Barry was sheepish. 'Mate, what could I do? She was OK, you know? She filled a spot and was really good with the kids.'

'Not so good with her colleagues, though, hey, Barry?'

'Well, Tony, she was never that popular, to be honest. She always had something to complain about. But I thought you'd be able to manage that. I mean, it wasn't that hard for me. If you just let her go on her merry way, she's happy. Her staff just kept their heads down and did whatever she told them to. She got terrific results with the students, and that made me look good.'

Tony nodded, not in agreement but in understanding. He couldn't believe his luck. Good old Barry had boldly thrown his dead cat over the fence.

How was Tony being bullied?

Susan came to the school with an expectation of special treatment. She had been expediently granted a privileged position in her previous role and had every expectation of her special untouchable status continuing. Susan began as she meant to continue, lashing out at existing staff members regardless of their positions in the school.

By undermining several members of Tony's teaching staff, then

Tony's deputy, and then Tony himself, Susan was employing the tactic of playing the victim. Her narcissistic nature meant she could never entertain the idea of herself being on the wrong side of any argument. As each level of authority failed to fall into line for Susan, she expanded her campaign, connecting to higher authority figures within the department and community to employ middle management squeeze strategies on Tony, his executive and classroom teachers.

Tony spent much of his time and energy on damage control rather than the leadership and management of his school.

What had Barry done wrong?

Barry knew that Susan's behaviours were unprofessional, yet he tolerated them to the extent that Susan was empowered to do whatever she liked without consequence. Barry was willing to have any number of his staff lose motivation and commitment to his school just because he was not prepared to call out and deal with the behaviours of an entitled bully. Eventually, Susan became someone else's problem, but Barry was complicit.

Lessons from Tony's story

Tony's caution in dealing with Susan was well founded. Tony should always listen to his gut feeling when inducting a new member of staff. He needs to be alert for potential issues when initial interactions seem out of step with what is required.

Getting on the front foot in meetings with entitled bullies is also an important practice for Tony to establish. He needs to get into a habit of hearing their concerns fully before considering if and when to comment. At any formal meeting wherein a support person is engaged, Tony needs to engage a reliable witness capable of writing accurate notes. He also needs to keep his own dispassionate, factual notes on everything that concerns him about Susan's ongoing behaviours. Such documentation will be extremely powerful when conduct (hers and his) is called to account. Susan's combative approach indicated no awareness of organisational conflict resolution procedures, which a more proactive Tony could have used to his advantage.

Tony must initiate discussions with his director, the education department, legal service and professional and ethical standards personnel as soon as practicable. He might also flag his concerns with the teachers' union, regardless of whether Susan is a member. Health and safety officers would also have a role to play in supporting Tony and his staff, including Susan. It's definitely a lot of work to properly set up these channels of communication, but Tony's thorough preparation in planning management processes will prevent an entitled bully from getting the upper hand in her attempts to discredit him. It will also prevent an escalation of Susan's poor behaviours and eliminate or minimise the psycho-social impact of her actions.

Tony has to take Susan's sick/stress leave at face value, being considerate of the advice of her treating doctor. He must not give Susan any opportunity to claim that he doubts her authenticity. In fact, she could be quite unwell, and there could be an avenue for Tony to support her mental health while concurrently improving the situation in her department in her absence.

The way forward

Downward, lateral and upward bullying are not mutually exclusive. Teaching staff who have developed a bullying habit will try to exert their influence wherever possible. However, if colleagues resist or block them in one direction, they may avoid those people and choose a softer target. We need to maintain the advantage of being on the front foot with meeting procedures, compliance and consultation to avoid the traps set by people who lash out in all directions.

Alert observation and accurate recording of the bully's claims and practices can assist us in developing a plan for managing them. It is time consuming and tedious to write up your many and varied encounters and observations in a logical and coherent format, but a written record can be absolute gold further down the track. While you can have no idea whether your upward bully is likewise recording every event and issue, with their own bias, a dispassionate, accurate record of interactions is indispensable in any formal meetings you have with and about your bully. Such records will also rebut any manufactured or differently recollected interactions or evidence presented.

Imagine this: You have a meeting with your bully, their support person, the federation representative[2] and your legal branch team member. You sit down, look every attendee in the eye and thank them with sincerity for their attendance. You place a bulky folder in front of you. You have a typed sheet of meeting notes on top, which is your script for running the meeting. At some early point in the proceedings, you open the folder to refer to the record of a relevant event. You scan through several documents on your way to the document you need. 'This is the one,' you smile and snap the tightly organised ring binder open, lay the document on the table in front of you, or hold it in lightly in your firm, steady hand, then read aloud in a calm and measured tone the clear, precise details of the issue you wish to refer to.

This technique is powerful. It takes away a great deal of uncertainty, gives structure to your meetings and confirms your power, both formal and informal, over the bullying member of staff. Preparation will pay off. Take the time to consult with your supervisors and potential support people early in the process rather than later. A senior legal advisor I know is fond of saying, 'Ring me. For goodness' sake, just ring and talk things through before you engage with your problem person. No one in my entire career has ever made their initial contact with me to say, "I ran a meeting yesterday with a really difficult member of staff. I was so pleased with the outcome that I just wanted to call to tell you how well it went".' She always gets a rueful laugh out of her audience for that one. It is not an admission of weakness to engage your supervisor, legal team, federation, occupational health and safety team, or brain trust. It is never a waste of your time or theirs. You will always learn something from them, and they will respect you for your willingness to let them help you. And just because you ask for advice, you are not obliged to take it; asking for advice allows you to consider more options than you thought you had. It's a great de-stressor, allowing you to concentrate on the task at hand rather than the personality causing the problem. When you can distance yourself from your emotions, you will make better decisions in dealing with bullies.

[1] Parent-Teacher Association (PTA) or Parent-Teacher Organization (PTO) (USA, Canada, UK)

[2] Teachers' union representative (USA, UK)

2

The warning signs

Upward bullying is an intense, frequent and aggressive manipulation of informal power in the workplace. Whether you are the head of a faculty, a deputy or a school principal, you will be subjected to attempts by some members of staff to bully you. No matter your skills, experience, reputation and ability, there will be staff members, be they teaching or support staff, who are motivated to bully you simply because you are their boss and they want to exert power over you.

Since the term 'bully' has come to popular usage, first in the playground and now in the workplace, the label has been unconsciously and deliberately misconstrued, overused and manipulated to suit the purpose of vexatious complainants. 'Bullying' is an emotionally loaded term and a complex concept, so it's important to have a shared understanding of what constitutes bullying in general and upward bullying in particular.

Schoolyard bullying has attracted recognition in education departments around the world with the intent of minimising its occurrence and impact. With increasing community acceptance that it's not acceptable to be a bully and plenty of resources allocated to this childhood problem, attention has turned to workplace bullying. When schoolyard bullies grow up, they do not necessarily grow out of their manipulative behaviours. Adult bullies have been recognised as the cause of significant damage to workplace practices and productivity and to their colleagues' physical, mental and emotional health. The fallout from unaddressed workplace bullying is always likely to be wide-ranging and expensive in terms of people, resources and productivity.

Academic researchers who have undertaken studies in various countries and cultures have agreed on what constitutes workplace bullying. Branch et al. 2004; Einarsen, 2000; Hadikin, R., & O'Driscoll, M., 2000; and Rayner et al. 2001 all provide detailed insights into the identified behaviours. However, scant research exists around the specific topic of upward bullying. While a number of academics who have researched bullying lament this situation, there has been no rush to respond to their recommendations for more targeted and extensive studies to explore, explain and analyse further the occurrences of upward bullying in the workplace, let alone specifically in the teaching profession.

For the purpose of this practical rather than theoretical book, these are some signs that you have been targeted by an upward bully in your school:

1. If you feel intimidated or harassed by a member of your staff or community.
2. If that person is repeatedly negative toward you in word or deed.
3. If you are being subjected to a power play by a subordinate colleague or member of the school community.

Intimidation or harassment

Intimidation or harassment may involve a staff member constantly demanding your attention to reverse a legitimate management decision you've made or to complain about not being consulted on a change to professional practice. This intimidation could take the form of long-winded, harping emails, the expectation of lengthy meetings where they take the opportunity to voice their contrary opinion at length and volume, or by deploying delegations of colleagues to express their concern about your ill-considered decision and incidentally intimate to you about how you've wronged their dear friend.

The casual observer or even long-term work colleague might not recognise the occurrence of bullying aimed at a senior colleague. They will not be privy to the minutiae of what is actually going on. Bullying is, by definition, a repeated attempt to cause harm. Attacks may be as subtle as a well-timed cough during an important presentation, a barbed comment disguised as humour or perceived ownership of a resource or program that affords that person informal power over their supervisor.

If the target is intimidated by such behaviour and is negatively affected by it, this truly is bullying behaviour, no matter how the casual onlooker may interpret it. Trying to downplay the seriousness with, 'She didn't mean it that way', or 'He's a really nice guy when you get to know his sense of humour' will have a negative rather than positive effect on the targeted person. 'No one believes me' or 'Maybe I'm being too sensitive' is the sort of negative self-talk that the bullied school leader might engage in, leading to self-guilt and serving no productive purpose. The bullied school leader may put on a brave face in an attempt to play down or fend off what to them is a debilitating attack, rattled by the fact that their more junior co-workers, their peers or even their supervisors don't share their reading of the situation. Ironically, their reluctance to seem vulnerable exposes their vulnerability through their reaction.

The ability of an upward bully to cloak their activities is usually a substantial factor in their success. It's not surprising that school leaders exposed to frequent and intensive acts of bullying can become weakened and worn down over time. As a target of upward bullying, you may register feelings of dread in standing up to your persecutor.

You may lose confidence in your abilities and second-guess decisions that you previously would have made without hesitation. You might even turn into your worst self, which could be anything from developing a debilitating illness to returning hostility with equal or even greater force. Both situations are no-win; ideally, you would hone your skills as an organisational leader to address each incident effectively and expediently with both strategic and systemic support lines to ensure your success and maintain your equilibrium.

Repeated negativity

There has been a general agreement among researchers that bullying is characterised by a substantial time period, usually cited as around six months of exposure to repeated negative acts. More recently, depending on the circumstances, I have seen some cautious acceptance that bullying may happen in a much shorter time frame and could even be traced to a single but highly debilitating event. In particular, when an upward bully enters a new school environment, they will start lashing out as they hit the ground because that is their accustomed habit for achieving whatever they want. It's worked for them to date, and they see no reason to change their ways (See Case Study #1: Lashing out in all directions).

Likewise, when a new principal arrives, bullying behaviours to 'put them in their place' and maintain the status quo may commence immediately. Keep in mind that the six-month guideline is not necessarily an accurate indicator of adult bullying. However, it is a measure of the seriousness of the problem when a target can evidence six months or more of intense and frequent aggression. That's a long time to suffer social and emotional abuse.

Heads of faculty, deputies and principals who are the target of subordinate bullies can be encouraged by colleagues above and below them to accept that managing such difficult workers is just one of the less savoury aspects of their leadership role— 'That's why you earn the big bucks'. Apprehensive school leaders may fail to disclose upward bullying practices because they are anxious about outing themselves as failing to command respect and are, therefore, potentially undeserving of a leadership role. 'Kiss up, kick down and don't complain' might well be the subtext in operation.

The extent of sniping and sabotage by upward bullies can be difficult to gauge, taking place in staff rooms, on playground duty or after hours when the bully feels most secure. In these situations, you'll likely get more of a sense of a pervading negative atmosphere than anything concrete to face head-on. When the upward bully is confident enough to be outspoken or dismissive in open forums, however, you know precisely who is firing the shots and who you need to deal with to take their illegitimate power away from them. This being said, it is reasonably common practice for a bully to hide behind one or several 'mouthpieces' who openly fire the bullets they secretly craft. In this case, it still won't take long to determine the common denominator.

Power play

Some bullies can be identified soon after you enter a new leadership role. During the initial days of assuming a promotional position, you can expect visits from various staff members under the pretence of providing assistance and guidance. However, their true intention is to assert their influence on your leadership and endeavour to shape your decisions according to their preferences. Others you will recognise when they challenge you in front of other members of staff, students or parents. A third group will have ensconced themselves in key roles which require specialist knowledge. Timetable managers, for example, hold expert knowledge but may be motivated by their desire for power and control rather than by the need to implement strategies that optimise student learning and staff deployment. If your chief timetable manager is holding their data close to their chest and insists that their way is the only way, that's a fair indication that you may need to install a new timetabling team and take power away from the incumbent, especially if the quality of the timetables is poor or unfairly favouring some staff members over others.

Some aggressive workers who bully the boss adroitly turn the tables when their unprofessional behaviours attract attention. When a teacher's supervisor shines a light on that worker's poor performance or inappropriate conduct, such bullies will often push back by claiming the victim status for themselves, claiming that the boss is bullying them.

It is not uncommon for an upward bully to make a formal complaint against their manager in order to hide their true colours, shifting attention and investigative energy away from themselves. Often, they'll take extended sick ('stress') leave, putting pressure on the school by their absence while affording themselves plenty of time to dig up 'evidence' against their principal, gather supporters and fire off letters and emails to various departmental officials.

In this situation, as well as dealing with the bully and their supporters daily, the targeted leader is unfairly compelled to justify (and question) their own actions. The bullied principal, deputy or head teacher, therefore, finds themselves as *the accused* by the person who has been making their life miserable AND being investigated by those who they should be able to look to for support. This practice is known as *middle management squeeze*, a situation wherein the bully's manager is squashed between the bully below them and the bully's sometimes unwitting but sometimes totally complicit supporters above them.

It is imperative to get on the front foot with your own supervisor regarding any strange feelings you may have about subordinate behaviours early in the piece. Having some background knowledge of an emerging situation from your perspective will help your manager avoid the trap of believing any complaint about you from your upward bully without any prior input from you. It is always better to bring your boss in early, ask their opinion, and consider their management strategies to assist you in working collaboratively and help you and your boss avoid nasty surprises.

Teachers or support staff members may apply subtle methods in their efforts to bully up. Specialist workers may withhold technical informa‐tion, as in the timetabling example above. They may fail to respond to requests expediently (or at all) by going slow, misunderstanding what was required, or withdrawing their specialist services. They may sabotage projects, sometimes by hiding physical paperwork or deleting online documents, or they might put out false information to change the direction of a planned program in order to derail it. If they have strong ties to other members of staff, they may enlist supporters to put pressure on their target while they play the puppeteer safely in the background. This last can result in *mobbing,* where an angry mob is provoked to attack an exposed target. Such mobs may lose sight of the original issue and attain a head of steam that takes on a life of its own. Many leaders have crumbled physically and mentally under the weight of the mob because their attacks can be multidirectional and unrelenting, often unexpected and therefore unprepared for.

The human cost

Although under-researched and barely acknowledged as a major prob‐lem for school leaders, upward bullying is easily recognised by those who have been targets of the practice and those in supportive roles. Upward bullying is characterised by workgroup conflicts, power imbal‐ances and challenges and thrives in dysfunctional physical or human environments. It creates an untenable situation for leaders who are diverted from their core business of educating children, and it can take a substantial toll on productivity and performance across the afflicted school.

Any member of a school's executive team may be a target of upward bullying, including the senior administrative officer, bursar or business manager who oversees clerical and other support staff. However, the school principal is in a particularly vulnerable situation, isolated from peer colleagues and expected to lead and manage each and every eventuality within their school. Upward bullies might hold positions as teachers, head teachers, deputies or non-teaching staff. Their targets could be any person in a supervisory position to them.

Despite prodigious evidence to the contrary, the actions of people who bully the boss are routinely dismissed as minor irritants and distractions. Therefore, the supervisor of an upward bully is most often tasked with dealing with bullying behaviours without a definitive playbook nor regulated support from their supervisors.

Upward bullying is deliberate, calculated and insidious. And as Big Tim fails to understand in Case Study #2, you cannot stop people from bullying you by giving them what they want.

Case Study #2: All things to all people

It didn't take too long for the ambulance to arrive. From the time Big Tim folded in on himself and collapsed untidily to the ground to when he was wheeled out to the waiting vehicle, strapped securely on the sturdy gurney, it could only have been around 15 minutes. But we all know that time moves slowly when life is at stake, and Jo breathed a heavy sigh of relief to see Tim, flat on his back but still alive, being driven with some urgency to their local hospital. His hand had been clammy to hold, his brow sweaty, his breath painfully shallow, and his colour a dull grey. He was obviously in deep discomfort, suffering agonising pains in his chest and limbs. At 55 years of age, overweight with a poor diet and little exercise, Tim was a man who surprised no one by having his first heart attack at work. Except that he didn't. Have a heart attack, I mean.

He was the jovial and popular primary school principal who loved the kids, made time for everyone, tried to solve every problem, and constantly cared and worried about his staff and school. He had always tried to be a peacemaker and a problem solver for his difficult and complex team, spending an inordinate amount of time looking after everyone and, in the end, unsurprisingly, pleasing no one. Everyone who had a gripe, an issue or an axe to grind complained to Tim, expecting him to fix it for them. And worse, they complained openly about him when they didn't get their way. This hurt Tim because he could see the good in everyone and wanted his team to be happy in their jobs. When his staff complained about him, he wanted to prove them wrong by winning each and every one of them over. He spent a crazy amount of time out of hours getting his own work done because he was in both formal and informal meetings with the sad, mad or bad people who manipulated him for most of the day. He had placated the many bullies on his team for years, and at last, his brain told his body, 'That's it, I can't take any more! I've had enough'.

As the ambulance disappeared around the corner, Jo gazed after it, concerned about her kind- and good-hearted friend. She thought about the many people who relied on him. She knew they would be devastated at his collapse and would realise, at last, how much their infighting had hurt him. And she was grateful that now they'd lay off him, give him a chance to get well and get on with his job. At least something good would come out of this near disaster.

Amazingly, Jo was wrong. When Tim returned to work, he barely got a chance to draw breath. It was business as usual for the workers competing for his attention and complaining about perceived injustices perpetrated or supported by Tim.

These debilitating panic attacks would plague Tim for the rest of his *working life. He would retire after five more fraught and increasingly fragile years—damaged, unfulfilled and with a brooding sense of guilt about what he had failed to achieve.*

How was Tim being bullied?

Several upward bullies recognised Tim as a target that they could easily manipulate. Competing factions monopolised Tim's time until managing issues between workers entirely clouded his outlook. He lost sight of his purpose as a school leader and had no work-life balance. Bullies lit spot fires all over the school and convinced Tim that it was his responsibility to deal with every single one. If Tim didn't perform to their satisfaction, any one of the bullies would lash out with complaints about him that they knew would get straight back to him and reset him on course to do their bidding.

What was Tim doing wrong?

Tim spent too much time on the wrong people and the wrong issues. Instead of quickly closing down petty arguments and insisting that his staff focus on their professional behaviours, he indulged them and attempted to befriend them. He enjoyed the feeling of popularity, of being the go-to person to solve everyone's problems. He lost focus on his leadership and management roles. Tim was all things to all people and, therefore, played into the hands of upward bullies by allowing them to set his agenda. He let his days be filled with time-wasting and circular arguments. He somehow knew this was wrong but could not work out how to haul himself out of the hole he had allowed others to dig for him. Ironically, he never asked for help; he could not let go of being the one person who would fix everything. Eventually, his mental health suffered to the point of collapse.

Lessons from Tim's story

A leader must set themselves up to earn respect rather than friendship. Not everyone will like us, nor should they be expected to. Tim needs to understand that such an important leadership role requires us to make unpopular decisions our staff may not understand or support. That's something we simply have to live with.

Tim could mitigate any backlash by explaining his vision and motivation for making decisions and moving on as necessary. Where he needs to change direction and employ flexibility going forward, he should be transparent in admitting errors and reasons for changes. It was not Tim's job as a school principal to make people happy; it was his job to create the conditions for a harmonious and productive workplace, which he was either unwilling or incapable of doing with the current staff. Tim must decide what and who deserves his time, effort and care. He also needs to value himself professionally and personally in this situation.

Going forward, Tim would be well advised to develop the conditions for distributed leadership across his middle management team. This would be the natural point to begin to empower others, build support structures and share the administrative burden.

The way forward

All school leaders can be subjected to attempts by their staff to bully them. Principals need to recognise and respond to staff aggression, intimidation and harassment, calling unacceptable behaviour for what it is: an aggressive manipulation of informal power. Like all bullies, teachers who bully their bosses can be challenging to stand up against. Accepting or ignoring their behaviour is not an option if you are to maintain your professional integrity and personal wellbeing.

You should never let an attempt to bully go unchallenged. Just like students, adults will push the boundaries until you show them your acceptable limits. If you are uncomfortable with how a staff member behaves towards you or others in front of you, you need to call it every time. Don't convince yourself that you've misheard or misunderstood; you can use feigning confusion to draw an upward bully into the open. 'Jean, that sounded like you were having a go at me. Did I understand you right when you said ...?' Jean might predictably respond with something like, 'I said it, but I didn't mean it' or 'Can't you take a joke?' to which you would reply in a similar vein to the way you would to some of your more challenging students, 'Jean, when you say something, I have to believe that you mean it' or 'It's not a joke unless everyone's laughing. That's not funny and not acceptable.'

It's hard at first. Not many of us are comfortable with calling out poor adult behaviour, and that's what bullies bank on: they will be free to escalate their intimidation and harassment unopposed. Bullies are the type of people who tend to enjoy conflict when they win, which is too often. By reacting in a timely and effective manner to the mean words and deeds of bullies, we can disarm them.

If you fail to challenge bullying behaviour, the next attack will come at you more strongly and confidently. If you are unsure about the motivation of deeds or words that cause upset, you still need to push back. The important thing to remember is to push back in a professional manner, not with a personal attack or a lack of confidence. If you have misjudged someone's motives, you maintain your power and dignity by employing a professional rebuttal of them. Going toe to toe makes it hard for anyone to work out who is the bigger bully, and you cause yourself and those around you unnecessary stress. You may need to rehearse these responses with a trusted colleague or even in the mirror to build confidence leading up to the event.

If you are new to a workplace or have been recently promoted within a school, the behaviours you see from colleagues in the first few days and weeks will likely be as good as they'll get. Unless, of course, you insist on better. Setting the bar gives everyone the boundaries they need. If you demand a standard from the outset, staff members will be much more likely to comply. If you ignore poor behaviours, they will get worse, more frequent and widespread, guaranteed.

There are always wonderful members of staff who want to wish you well on your appointment, get to know a bit about you and ease your transition to the school they love. They are altruistic, generous and genuine. However, among the first handful of people to make a beeline for your office over your first week, some are definitely there to check out your vulnerability. They seek out your weak spots and develop their plans to manipulate you. They often turn up when you're a bit distracted and take advantage of the opportunity to get under your guard. A welcoming smile and an offer to help you understand how 'things work around here' aren't often what you'd like them to be. Be alert and more than slightly alarmed but bring your poker face to the game. A helpful strategy to remind such folk of their place in the pecking order is to greet their unexpected arrival, then ask them to sit and wait until you are ready to speak to them—around 10 minutes should suffice—and then invite them into your office space and initiate your chat without distractions. In this way, you immediately take control of the situation, showing your caller that you are in charge and not at their beck and call.

Another important tip to send a strong message is to ensure you set up your office space to show that you own the space. Your desk and the private area behind it should take up most of your office. You should face the door in order to see who is approaching you, and so they can see you noticing them. Resist the temptation to set up comfortable visitor chairs and an egalitarian workspace. If the space is too welcoming, you will have a line of a particular type of staff member at your door at any given time looking for their chance to sprawl on your armchairs, set their coffee on your side table and unload their thoughts and feelings on a surprisingly vast and time-consuming range of topics. You have better things to do with your time, as do they.

Chapter 3 will unpick some of the perplexing complications and contradictions around upward bullying. The more we know about upward bullying, the better we can focus our efforts to address the issue for ourselves and support our fellow school leaders.

3

Complications and contradictions

While this book has been written as a working guide for practical purposes, to understand the mysteries and misconceptions around upward bullying more fully, it will be helpful for us to look into the findings of the existent research, which testifies to the paradoxical nature of upward bullying.

To complete my masters degree, I undertook a literature review of worldwide research into upward bullying. There wasn't much out there, but those academics who had delved into upward bullying were passionate about their research and determined to light the way for increased knowledge, understanding and support in adult bullying situations.

For my thesis, I interviewed several educational directors, tapping into their extensive knowledge and experience of working at all levels in a wide variety of schools during their careers and in their current senior executive roles as line managers of school principals. Although none of my participants had heard the term 'upward bullying' prior to agreeing to an interview with me, all of them quickly recognised the phenomenon in our discussion, and they required no prompting to recall serious cases of upward bullying they had witnessed or been subjected to.

The literature I reviewed and the participants I interviewed agreed that upward bullying does not receive the recognition it warrants. There was a universal agreement: to deal more effectively with the problem, we need to know more about it.

A lack of knowledge

While upward bullying tends to be underreported, for reasons I'll explore later, downward bullying appears to be over-reported and over-anticipated. Several studies I analysed as part of my academic research used a version of self-referral for data collection and tended to ask loaded questions, which lent themselves towards identifying bullying bosses rather than other bullies in the workplace. For example, in their 2012 study, *Bullying of Staff in Schools*, Riley, Duncan and Edwards deployed a questionnaire that put 44 questions to participants about bullying scenarios in the teaching workplace. Of these, 28 related to hierarchical positions within the school that assumed bullying was connected to a formal power imbalance. They ignored the impact of informal power bases in the workplace. For instance, statements that required a graded response are all skewed towards identifying downward bullying, such as:

1) Tasks are set with unreasonable or impossible targets or deadlines.

2) Your concerns about unfair treatment, bullying and harassment are dismissed.

3) Recognition, acknowledgement and praise are withheld.

Unfortunately, this survey and others similar to it lack the appetite for capturing valid data to identify upward bullying. Researchers who have opened the lid on upward bullying have estimated the prevalence to be somewhere between 10% in Namie and Namie's *US Workplace Bullying Survey* of 7740 participants (2007) and 33% in Mintz-Binder & Calkins Australian study of 77 Nursing Directors (2012). That's a huge difference in results, but even 10% is a significant number, partly because we know upward bullying to be under-reported and partly because of the ratio of teaching staff to principals. As the target of upward bullying is always a leader or manager, the shockwaves of upward bullying reach extensively across the workplace, disempowering leadership and disrupting core business, resulting in tainting students' education experience and undermining school communities.

Where researchers have identified upward bullying in the workplace, female workers were discovered to be the perpetrators of bullying towards male bosses more often than in any other configuration. Male bosses were also the least likely to complain of being bullied, perhaps fearful of being seen as weak and unsuitable for their managerial role or from a fear of damaging their future promotional prospects. You can read more about this topic from Sarah Branch and her associates in their 2004 *Perceptions of upwards bullying: An interview study*, and from Fiona Lee in her intriguingly titled 1997 paper, *When the going gets tough, do the tough ask for help? Help seeking and power motivation in organizations.*

These researchers and others found that male bosses tend to shy away from making complaints about female workers for fear of being tangled up in a fraudulent accusation of sexist or sexual behaviour. One of the participants in my M.Ed. research made a salient observation that females tend to be more connected socially than males and, therefore, may use their social contacts to initiate mobbing behaviours, which he had seen on two occasions perpetrated by female antagonists but never by males. Having said that, it could simply be the case that there have always been more female classroom teachers than males and traditionally, more men have attained school leadership roles than women, though the balance at the top, at least, is changing. In primary schools, it is still commonplace that one of the few, if not only, male staff members will be the school principal. (The other one is likely to be the groundskeeper.)

Across schools, upward bullying has been identified much more often in high schools, arguably because primary teachers are more relationship driven and less federation (union) oriented. Primary teachers tend to focus on their love for their kids, and secondary teachers on their love of subject areas. In primary schools, where communities play a more active and confident role in their children's education, parents and community groups might be more likely to bully the principal than teachers.

A lack of understanding

To date, upward bullying in the teaching profession has been largely unacknowledged, undervalued and unaddressed. This points to a lack of understanding of the stresses inflicted on school leaders at both senior and middle management levels. There are times, for example, when managers try to enforce unpopular work practices because they are attempting to implement new policies, whether their own or those mandated by the department. This results in bullies intent on resisting change and asserting dominance over their managers. Heads of teams and, to a lesser extent, deputies and assistant principals seem to be targeted more in this situation, known as *middle management squeeze*. They are pressured from above to get their team to perform and from below as a calculated act of resistance and emotional abuse (Ariza-Montes et al. 2014). A principal, deputy or team leader is in a very tricky position when simultaneously attempting to shield and defend themselves from unwarranted attacks while at the same time contesting malicious claims of downward bullying made against them. The workplace grievance process can be long and gruelling and may be abused to prevent disciplinary action or mediation by a manager in dealing with upward bullies.

As recognition of workplace bullying increases and with it the structures and processes to combat it, it is ironic that the declaration of having been bullied by a boss can be used as a weapon by which an upward bully can turn the tables on their target, hiding behind the protection of workplace structures and norms.

The targeted school leader may weaken under pressure, second guess themselves or lose motivation to do their job well. Sometimes, without the ability or willingness to self-reflect or seek guidance, a school leader may resort to heavy-handed response tactics, returning fire with fire and resulting in what has been coined a *spiral of incivility*, which you can read more about in *Tit for Tat? The Spiralling Effect of Incivility in the Workplace* (Andersson, L. M., & Pearson, C. M. 1999).

The difficulty or even impossibility of managing malicious complaints means that sometimes the school leader simply has to wait out the complainant, and resolution only occurs when one or more parties leave that worksite. A besieged deputy may abandon their position because they could see no other way to end the conflict. A worn-down principal may be removed and replaced by their line manager. They may retire early, choosing health over wealth and causing the department to lose their skills and experience because the bullying behaviours were not adequately addressed. A bully might move on because they have lost traction, or they could be relocated against their will. All such cases take an inordinate amount of time and effort and an excessive toll on the target, their loved ones and the wider school community.

Without strongly enforced policies and procedures to address upward bullying, incivility can mutate into a more intense revenge and conflict cycle between the target and the aggressor, affecting the entire school community. Of course, it never ends well. Perhaps this is not always the case for the upward bully, but on absolutely every occasion, it is the case for the school leader who takes the bait and loses their professional edge.

Mobbing of a target occurs when an upward bully 'recruits' teachers both in and outside their faculty, middle executive, parents, community and even students to their cause. Some observers suggest that mobbing may be the ramping up of aggression orchestrated by a successful upward bully. A converse view is that mobbing occurs when the upward bully does not feel strong enough to stand alone against a principal or other targeted supervisor. Probably both observations are correct. The senior executive members interviewed for my thesis were very familiar with the raising of a mob and used emotively charged terms including 'rampage', 'lynch mob' and 'the Frankenstein analogy' to describe mobs they had seen. They spoke of teachers and middle executive members who rallied to mob behaviours to punish principals they judged as inadequate. A typical context that gives rise to a mob is whereby staff behaviours are entrenched, and they justify their bullying by calling it 'standing up for my rights' or getting rid of a person 'who can't be here when they're not doing the right job for us'.

One-on-one, principals should have the skills to manage an individual bully, contingent on what other issues they have to deal with at the time. However, when a teacher bully manages to manipulate those around them into a mob, the principal can become too worn down to oppose them or too oblivious to the machinations of the bully to join the dots and realise what they have been drawn into. We'll discuss mobs more in Chapter 6.

A lack of support

Where the target of an upward bully lacks support, the power base tips drastically in favour of the subordinate staff member. A principal who feels insecure in, dissatisfied with or frustrated by a job that can be extremely emotionally demanding may exhibit vulnerability to which the upward bully is finely attuned. This vulnerability is compounded when a school leader does not have a strong familial or social support network. Speaking out about being bullied by a member of staff takes courage and confidence. More vulnerable targets, however, try to manage such a bully without asking for help, attempting to deal with 'their own rubbish' rather than appear 'soft' or 'weak'. This is ironic because by not asking for help early in the conflict, the target opens themselves up to increased severity of bullying in addition to the likely investigation of their own practices from above. Once such an investigation is initiated, it can be challenging for those undertaking the analysis to accurately read the situation and determine how to best proceed. It can then be difficult to distinguish between a target and a perpetrator. At this point, there's probably some culpability on both (or all) sides and truths may easily be blurred. Rather than feel supported by their managers in this situation, the bullied boss comes under even more pressure to explain themselves and the actions or inactions they've taken in isolation.

Many education systems protect the subordinate aggressor, especially where that person calls in union support, invokes health and safety concerns or takes stress-related sick leave, further disempowering the targeted leader and drawing out the conflict for an extended time.

Unless school leaders also seek support, they will be on the back foot. The lack of knowledge and understanding of the phenomenon drives the lack of support for targets of upward bullying. School leaders need to be able to identify bullying issues more rapidly and ask for help to deal with them from the outset. Requesting your immediate supervisor assist you in dealing with bullies on your staff is not weak. It is prudent to put your line manager in the loop so that they understand your issues as they unfold, reticent as you may be to do so.

I would suggest that we need a paradigm shift. Rather than fearing that our complaints would lead to an accusation of us not doing our jobs properly, we school leaders should insist on our supervisors' early involvement to assist us in managing bullies in our schools. Knowing that some upward bullies will disdain the authority of their supervisors, leaping over their managers in an attempt to gain the support of more senior executives, we need to get in first in a proactive and professional rather than a reactive manner. That's why building a good rapport with our immediate supervisors is vital to our role as school principals. Sometimes it's not easy or even the most palatable part of the job, but principals need to be able to effectively manage up as well as manage down. It's much more pleasant to consider tactics regularly with a supervisor or mentor than to be called in cold to an unexpected meeting with your senior manager to 'please explain' an allegation against you.

Principals, assistant principals, deputies, faculty heads and team leaders must have the confidence to speak out earlier rather than later and be transparent about the aggression they suffer from teacher colleagues and other subordinate members of their school community. When the practice of upward bullying is recognised and understood by the wider school community, support can be more readily accessed to benefit system-wide improvements. By raising possible or actual incidences of upward bullying as early as practicable, you can sound the situation out, and the worst-case scenario will be that you are misreading the situation. However, in that case, your boss will appreciate that you respect them and seek their wisdom, unless you have an attack of the boy who cried wolf, which will eventually wear a bit thin for anyone in a supervisory role. That's where developing a brains trust—people you can sound out concerns with in a safe environment before you take it up to your boss—can be invaluable.

Case Study #3: A work in progress

'Got a few minutes for me, Ian?'

Tom had suddenly appeared in the doorway, looking a bit anxious, pretty rattled in fact, Ian thought. Ian put aside the textbook he'd been considering for the new junior music syllabus. He invited Tom into his office and closed the door.

'How'd you go?'

Tom sighed heavily as he sank down opposite Ian. 'It started off reasonable, then it sort of faltered and fell off the rails a bit.'

'OK, let's go through it step by step.'

Ian was Tom's peer mentor and had been for almost a year. The principal of Southside High School had asked Ian to support Tom after it became obvious that Tom needed to develop his interpersonal skills more fully to help him in his staff management role. Ian and Tom met every fortnight to discuss Tom's evolving skills in handling some pretty headstrong staff, including Melanie, the school's long-serving and highly opinionated Physics teacher.

Tom was about to describe his latest faculty meeting, which he had called solely to distribute teaching allocations for next year. It was a new tactic for Tom. Ian had convinced him it was a tried-and-true way to maximise transparency and collegial acceptance of why and who got what to teach.

'I got there early and made sure that all the classroom chairs were rearranged at the front of the room around a single table so Mel couldn't hide up the back and mutter stuff I couldn't hear.'

'Good work. Did you send out an agenda beforehand?'

'Yep, everyone had a chance to read up on it well before they arrived, and I clued up a couple of reliable people with more details so they could back me up if someone asked strange questions.'

'But you didn't send out their individual timetables in advance?'

'No, everyone got to see their own and each other's at the exact same time, so they could compare and make any comments in front of the whole faculty as you suggested.'

'Well done. Did you have a bit of a chat with each person as they came in?'

'I sure did. I even got Peter talking about the concert he and Mel went to that their daughter was singing at. He was really friendly, but Mel was the same old sourpuss, couldn't even say hello but launched into another

complaint about her workload, so I cut her short and didn't have much to say to her.'

Ian frowned a little, made a note for a later coaching point with Tom and encouraged him to continue, 'Right, what next?'

'I got Peter to do the minutes so I could have a written record, like you suggested. And to keep him focused on the meeting rather than watching Mel rolling her eyes at him whenever I said something she didn't like.'

'And did that go OK for you?'

'Well, yes and no. Let's just say Peter isn't the best minute-taker in the world. He kept getting caught up in the conversation and forgetting to write down the important bits. I had to remind him about six times to write stuff down.'

'But did it stop him doing the eye-rolling stuff with Mel?'

'Definitely no eye rolling, but just 20 minutes in, after I'd put the allocations up for everyone to compare with each other's, she was yelling at me that I was picking on her, that I didn't appreciate her expertise, and it was unfair.'

'How did you respond to that?'

'I tried the stonewall tactic you taught me. I nearly lost my nerve when she kept coming back at me, louder and louder. But I stuck to it, and eventually, she went all quiet. It was a bit eerie. It kind of changed the atmosphere in the room. I was shaking a bit, and my voice was wobbly, so I took a few deep breaths to pull myself together. The notes I wrote myself for what I needed to cover really helped me get back on track while I calmed down. And that response you suggested worked really well.'

Ian smiled, 'Which response was that?'

''Where she just wouldn't let up and kept on and on. I let her run for a bit so everyone could see the way she carries on, then I said, "Mel, unfortunately, you and I will have to agree to disagree on this", and she had nowhere to go; it really stopped her in her tracks.'

'Great work. It's hard, mate, but you can't take it personally. It'll get easier the more you practise. You need to try out a few tactics, make some mistakes

and gain some confidence. Be kind to yourself. I'm guessing Mel didn't quite leave it alone; what did she try next?'

'At one point, she did say that she wouldn't be helping Kim at all with her Year 11 Physics class. Kim actually looked a bit relieved by that statement, to be honest. And when I'd finished the meeting and asked for any further questions or comments, she just sighed, gathered up all her stuff, and stomped out.'

'Right,' Ian grinned, 'so it went much better than last year.'

'Well, yes. Comparatively speaking.' Tom's shoulders slumped a bit. 'But will it ever go without a drama from Mel?'

'Tom, I'm not promising miracles; let's just treat it as a work in progress.'

The previous year, without the wise counsel of his peer mentor, Tom had put a lot of effort into a balanced timetable for his staff. He allocated everyone a senior class, ensuring that all specialist subjects, particularly Physics, Chemistry and Biology, were shared and that everyone had their fair share of the difficult classes. He was proud of his effort; whichever way he shone a light onto his allocations, they came out equitably. They made perfect sense, and he knew he couldn't do it any better. Done and dusted, he emailed each member of staff their individual allocations and turned his attention to room allocations.

A very long email at 10.30 pm caught his attention. It was from Melanie. And boy, was she cranky.

Tom, [No greeting, he noticed, but that wasn't unusual. Mel's default position was abrasive.]

You have made big mistakes on my timetable that you need to fix. I have not taught junior science for over 10 years, and I will not teach junior science. I am not a junior science teacher; I only teach Physics and have done so for the last 12 years at this school. My results speak for themselves, and I am hurt that you have taken me off a Year 11 Physics class without consultation with me. Who have you put on this class? If it is Kim, she does not have the qualifications or experience to give those students what they

need to get through the senior course. Kim was a student teacher of mine six years ago, and I know her very well. She has never taught Physics and is not ready to start now.

[The email continued for some time in this vein, giving depth and detail into Kim and Tom's professional and personal inadequacies.]

I work harder than anyone else at this school and am your best teacher. You are not giving me the respect I deserve, and I suspect it's because I'm a woman, and it's obvious you don't like capable women. You just want to tell us all what to do, and we jump when you demand it. There has been no communication, as usual, about the faculty allocations. I will not be treated this way.

Melanie Johnstone

Tom was shaken by the vitriol Mel expressed about him, not just professionally but personally. She'd really misunderstood him and his intentions. What if he got branded as a misogynist? He had to defend himself but also assert his right to tell her exactly what classes she'd be taking and why. He had to push back strongly, or she'd think he was weak. He had to shut this down before he got a reputation for not being able to handle his own staff. Class allocation was, after all, his decision, not Mel's, and he had to make her understand that she was obliged to comply with his directions. He emailed her back, drafting and redrafting his long email, eventually hitting send at 12.15 am.

Mel, [He mirrored her abrasive tone.]

I'm sorry that you don't understand how allocation works. I'm happy to explain it to you, but it will take some time that neither of us have right now. See below why I need more than one person on Physics at our school and why I need you to teach junior science from now on ...

Of course, sleep evaded him after that. Bleary-eyed and sick to the stomach, he sought Mel out before school the next day. He ran into her coming out of the principal's office. His stomach sank even further when Mel simply brushed past him, and his boss Jasmine invited him into her office, then closed the door.

'Tom,' Jasmine began, 'we need to talk about how you've managed your staffing allocations.'

How was Tom being bullied?

Melanie had carved out a comfortable niche for herself over a number of years as the sole Physics teacher in the school. She was a custom and practice bully, digging her heels in around change processes. She was the owner of knowledge as the self-anointed expert in her chosen field and had no intention of giving up that informal power base. She had no respect for Tom's authority as her supervisor and no compunction in going right to the top, engaging Jasmine, the school principal, in her dispute in a classic attempt at middle management squeeze.

What had Tom done wrong?

Tom mistakenly assumed that his staff would defer to his formal power as their head of faculty. He thought that by organising an equitable timetable and sending it out via individual emails, they would simply comply with what, to him, was a well-thought-out and balanced distribution of teacher loads.

In working alone, Tom made (at least) two mistakes. Firstly, the work he'd initially done on staff allocations was inward looking. We always need more than one pair of eyes on complex issues to see things from a different perspective, and they should belong to someone who is neutral and has a different way of looking at problems from our own. Secondly, Tom ducked the opportunity to have potentially difficult conversations with each member of his staff. If he had done so, he would have known where each of them was concerning what they taught, where their qualifications lay and what they aspired to teach. Tom assumed too much, including that everyone's logic and motivations were similar to his. Cobbled up with this assumption was the fear of being wrong. If he had canvassed opinions, he might have felt the need to change some of his decisions, which he thought would show him as a weak leader.

Tom took Melanie on toe to toe and sent a reactive email without giving himself time to cool down or consult with someone who could provide dispassionate advice. His tone, unfortunately, mirrored hers. Being polite and respectful must always be the leader and manager's default tone. A professional tone sends a powerful message, modelling how members of staff should address one another, and the tone cannot be called into question in any arena in which it is aired.

As a member of the management team, Tom should never respond to an out-of-hours email. He could draft an email, perhaps seeking input from a mentor and have it off his mind for the evening and ready to go, but he needs to press 'send' in or close to regular office hours. This is the power position. Such a considered response implies that he is not reading emails late into the night and does not exist simply to make members of his staff happy.

How Tom was supported

Tom's principal, Jasmine, was able to point out the error of Tom's manage-ment tactics to him and buddy him up with an emotionally intelligent peer faculty head he was willing and able to learn from. She recognised that Tom needed time and guidance to develop a more measured approach to managing his staff, whether difficult or not. Ian was well chosen as he could relate to Tom as a critical friend. Tom respectfully took on Ian's advice and tried out strategies Ian put to him. By developing a trustful, professional atmosphere, Ian was able to encourage Tom and illuminate mistakes he made along the way, e.g., when Tom failed to connect with Melanie at the start of his faculty meeting. Ian taught Tom strategies to unite his team during meetings (around a central table), to engage in valued conversation (having a staff member take minutes) and to develop empathy for each other (giving equitable timetables out to all members of staff at the same time to foster transparency and professional discussion).

Lessons from Tom's story

As leaders and managers, you need to seek out and regularly consult a critical friend to help you analyse and evaluate your actions and the reactions of staff. Getting caught up in the moment and being pulled into a war of incivility that masks the way forward is easy. To avoid this trap, you have to be mindful of how you come across to others and where the holes in your planning and preparation might be. Considered reflection is important and is almost impossible to do alone. Your mentor should be someone who can guide and critique your actions, someone you can trust to be honest and frank with and who can see situations from a different perspective than your own.

You can learn tactics such as stonewalling to defuse an upward bully in a group situation and show you're a strong leader, not only in the mind of the bullying teacher but also in the minds of the bystanders and potential mob members on your staff.

The way forward

The waters get muddied around the concept of upward bullying, and this is due to a lack of recognition of the existence of the problem, coupled with a lack of understanding and support for the target. While bullying *by* the boss is undisputed, bullying *of* the boss has been glossed over, partly due to how perpetrators operate and partly to how targets respond to being bullied by their staff members.

Fewer and fewer teachers are putting their hands up for promotion. Those who attain promotional positions often lament that the most pressing demands of the job were not the reason they came into the profession. Philip Riley's longitudinal principal wellbeing surveys highlight the emotional demands that often drive many principals to leave their jobs. It's not that they are necessarily ready to leave, but rather they feel compelled to escape the intense pressure of the situation. Offensive behaviour by members of staff has contributed enormously to leadership stress, with the rate of adult bullying of managers over four times higher in schools than in other workplaces. This situation cannot continue if we are to attract and retain quality practitioners at the executive level.

To effect change in the behaviours of others, we need to change what we're doing. The prevalence of upward bullying has to be acknowledged at both an individual and system-wide level. We have to gain skills in identifying what constitutes upward bullying and how to deal with it effectively. We must extend reactive and proactive support for school leaders to manage adult bullies in schools. Dealing with difficult members of staff should not be viewed as just part of the job or 'the reason you get the big bucks'. We take bullying of classroom teachers and support staff very seriously. Executive members of staff must be given the same consideration. If all school executives were trained in recognising and managing adult bullies; if interventions existed and were judiciously employed; and if crisis management personnel were deployed as needed, then we would surely retain more good people and promote more positive and productive workplace environments.

Grumbling about the principal is an international sport and tolerated as a way of letting off steam, but the upward bully takes discontent with school leadership to a whole new level. Upward bullies are not at all respectful of nor deterred by formal power. Chapter 4 explores the nature and motivations of the type of people who have no hesitation in taking on authority figures in their workplace.

4

Justified and entitled

Anyone who has been in a leadership position for a considerable time understands that grumbling about the boss is a popular pastime. It goes with the territory that whatever we do is subject to intense scrutiny, criticism and debate. These are, after all, the hallmarks of professional staff focused on continuous improvement. However, while some staff habitually participate in the grumbling, the vast majority get on with what is required of them with reasonably good grace. The upward bully, however, can be relied upon to ramp up the discontent with their boss exponentially.

There are two types of upward bullying in the teaching profession. The first has always been with us, and the second is emerging, arguably a product of the modern age of narcissism. (For more on the modern egotistic society, see Jean Twenge and Keith Campbell's *The Narcissism Epidemic*). Neither type of bully is insecure nor suffers from low self-esteem. They do not secretly admire nor envy the leadership abilities of their chosen targets, nor do they want to emulate them. These perceived characteristics are all well-meaning myths that actually prevent us from dealing effectively with bullies who are either justified or entitled. Both types are self-righteous and aggressive.

Commonalities

Whether you are confronted with a justified (custom and practice) bully or a member of the emerging entitled set, the member of staff trying to bully the boss will employ tactics that are indicators of high rather than low self-esteem. Aggression and anger are common, often inconsistent with the size of the issue they are concerned about, reminiscent of a toddler tantrum. They will display limited or even no desire to admit mistakes, avoiding accurate self-reflection in a true narcissistic style. Attempts to elicit empathy are unlikely to achieve a positive result. Upward bullies apply pushback against and avoidance of mediation processes and disciplinary action. They use oppositional strategies against their perceived enemy in order to take any investigative focus away from themselves and reposition it onto their target.

Confidence is strong in an upward bully. These people have sometimes been described as having a 'game' mentality, relishing opportunities to erode the formal power of their boss through overt or passive aggression, often both. Dismissive of formal power, upward bullies may fail to attend meetings, withhold key information or spread spiteful gossip, resulting in the professional and social exclusion of their target. It is not uncommon for a teacher bullying the boss to embark on a formal grievance proceeding to take the heat off their own behaviours and divert the energies of their principal to defend themselves against malicious complaints.

It is a forlorn hope to appeal to the better nature, sense of fair play or moral integrity of an upward bully. These people actively enjoy conflict and thrive on disharmony. It is not their goal to resolve issues. They strive to create chaos in which they can act as they please and enjoy the mayhem they have orchestrated. It's a power trip.

Might upward bullies have serious personality disorders? It would stand to reason. Given the lack of empathy such bullies display, there could be a link to narcissism, borderline personality disorder or even sociopathy. While some of the current academic literature makes passing mention of such disorders, there has as yet been no definitive research undertaken into possible links between upward bullying and personality disorders.

We must remember that, as school leaders, we are not clinicians. We need to focus on managing the behaviours as they present to us rather than second-guessing the reasons for them. Teachers who cannot or will not agree with or accept the reasonable and considered viewpoint of a person with higher authority are a serious problem for us. Such bullies will work towards reversing or subverting decisions made above them. A staff member who harbours resentment towards a more successful colleague will look for any and all ways to bring that person down professionally, socially and emotionally. A person with an agenda that does not align with educational values will damage progress for continuous improvement in a school. These are typical motivations for the bullies we can identify on our staff, and these people may fall into one or both of two categories.

The justified bully

This custom and practice bully will resist any changes to their daily routine, rationalise their unprofessional behaviour by citing convention, clinging to 'this is the way we've always done it' and 'I know that might work in other places, but that won't work here'.

Justified bullies are comfortable with the status quo. They will resist changes that take their security and routine away. This person may be a long-term staff member at the school they attended as a student. They lay claim to the school as their personal territory. They are convinced that while changes may have been made in other schools, this school is running just fine the way it is. They are the type of people who love rules to keep students and colleagues in line; the more punitive and numerous, the better, just so long as they can inflict these rules at will on other people. For themselves, however, the goalposts are very bendy indeed. They rarely take a backward step, and they never admit fault. They are masters of the passive voice — 'The assignment for Year 7 hasn't been written yet', rather than 'I didn't get the Year 7 assignment written on time'. They also profess to be too busy at all times and are self-rated as 'the best' and 'most hard-working' member of staff (a claim their best friend or spouse, also members of staff, will back up in case you require any extra proof).

The challenge becomes apparent when a leader aims to transform the school's culture and practices, which could involve altering rules, such as a school principal who wants to foster self-regulation and independent responsibility among students and staff. Such a leader will run into hostile opposition led by this entrenched bully whose tactics have worked on leaders of the past. If this person is not managed expediently, they will sabotage any move towards improving the workplace. Justified bullies tend to be those who have been in the workplace for a long time, building up a sphere of influence, partly made up of sycophants, partly of bystanders and partly of people who avoid crossing them due to their long-term informal power in the community. Members of these three groups make up the mob for the custom and practice bully to mobilise as necessary to push back against any changes initiated by leaders and managers.

Justified bullies are people who are unwilling or unable to agree with the opinions of those with formal power over them. Indeed, regardless of position, they tend not to accept anyone's opinion that may differ from theirs. They often have a subversive agenda to their official role statement and have engineered to have a comfortable life untroubled by the actual requirements of their job, which they choose to view as optional or advisory rather than mandatory. Often, these people develop close ties to their union representatives to attempt to manipulate and misuse federation support. It is not uncommon for a custom and practise upward bully to be the school's long-term union representative because other members of staff will not dare to challenge them for the role.

As difficult as pushback bullies are, they can be changed, and often, they are actually well-respected and competent teachers with core beliefs that originated in a love of teaching and learning and genuine concern for kids. They're just not adept at sharing the limelight, appreciating the talents of their colleagues, or accepting the authority of their principal and other school leaders. And they don't like being drawn out of their comfort zone. Changing their practice could even be tantamount to admitting incompetence. With careful and considered ongoing management, they can sometimes respond to well-planned and executed consultation, mediation and disciplinary procedures initiated by their supervisors.

Unfortunately, that is not the case with the entitled bully.

The entitled bully

Entitled staff members can, in their own minds, do no wrong. They do not accept criticism or willingly tolerate active supervision. They have little self-concept and lack the ability to reflect on their actions. They are predisposed to malicious and aggressive behaviour in response to reasonable attempts to manage unacceptable workplace behaviours, and terms such as 'vile' and 'vitriol' have been used to describe their manner of interaction with well-intentioned supervisors. The degree of hostility such bullies may generate when their behaviours are challenged can be well out of proportion to what the situation would seem to demand.

Fuelled by unshakeable self-righteousness, the entitled bully genuinely believes that their attacks on their boss are justified, as they consider themselves superior to the individual in a formal position of power above them. Somewhat surprisingly, these bullies are emerging not so much from the ranks of younger teachers but are more often older members of staff or mature-age converts to the teaching fraternity.

It is a myth that bullies attack those they most want to be like—popular and successful leaders—due to underlying low self-esteem; the opposite is actually the case (Branch et al. 2004). Entitled bullies do not recognise fault in anything they do, and they put serious effort into eroding the credibility of those who do not share their opinion of themselves. While entitled bullies may begin their campaign with one-on-one tactics against a leader, they will not hesitate to engage a mob of supporters or appeal to powers above their supervisor to expand the attack to a number of fronts. When they fire up fellow staff members or even middle managers to attack the target on their behalf, this is less due to a perceived lack of confidence and more in line with the bully's perception of themselves as a puppeteer or the brains behind the operation. Enlisting the support of the leader's boss (middle management squeeze) indicates supreme confidence and control, and it's a tactic that can work extremely well to take the managerial heat off the entitled bully. This strategy can be devastating and even career-ending for the unprepared target of the entitled upward bully.

A typical example of the actions of an entitled bully at the deputy or assistant principal level is when a new leader is 'parachuted' into a principal role in a school. This will result, however briefly, in staff and community members feeling cheated of the opportunity to choose their new school principal. The person coming in is viewed with suspicion, especially if newly arrived in the local community.

Prior to the appointment of that new principal, the substantive deputy or assistant principal had filled the role, and regardless of how well they did the job, they had assumed that the job was rightly theirs. So, naturally, when a new principal is appointed, the conditions become ideal for upward bullying behaviours to emerge. The second in command can usually call on a broad power base and an extensive knowledge of structures, procedures, relationships and motivations within the school community that the new principal has limited understanding of. The 'white anting' of a new principal by their deputy is one of the most often reported scenarios of upward bullying in schools, according to the participants in my M.Ed. study and the wider discussions I have held with my peers. As the name suggests, 'white anting' involves the systematic and subversive undermining of the targeted leader, who may still look intact from the outside but is hollowed out within.

One of my thesis participants spoke of a deputy who would sabotage the work of a principal by refusing to 'follow through with things they were told to and then they just shrug their shoulders'. Another spoke resignedly of how a principal was overtly challenged, even openly defied by their deputy 'if the principal was away for a day, they'd reverse a decision and determine that they weren't doing something anymore'. Timetable managers might construct subject lines so that subjects or specialist teachers are disadvantaged. Deputies might prioritise real or fabricated meetings over attending student altercations in the classroom or playground.

Social exclusion is another powerful tool the upward bully uses to erode the support base of their principal target. One of my participants spoke of bullies being 'free to run their mouth off at will ... widening and sowing doubts about capacity' of their principal, whereas the hapless target was bound to abide by professional standards of workplace conduct, leaving them isolated and vulnerable. It should be said that this perception does not have to be a reality. Bullies are only 'free' if the leader lacks the knowledge or strength to manage these behaviours.

In such a situation, the targeted leader is in danger of emotional overload in dealing with an entitled bully who is relentless in their attacks, energised by their surety of purpose. If a bully is disgruntled at being overlooked for promotion, it is reasonable to assume that they and their supporters will not be working to capacity, which impacts badly on the leadership and management capabilities of the principal. Sooner or later, management at a higher level will be involved in investigating why the school isn't running as it should. Naturally, the investigations will start at the principal level. At this point, the entitled upward bully will have plenty of 'evidence' to support their complaint that the wrong person was chosen for the principal job they continue to covet. At this point, it can all go terribly wrong for the embattled school leader.

Case Study #4: Kathy's Dream Job

Kathy was delighted. All her hard work had paid off, and after five years as a principal in a small rural school where she'd learned the ropes, she had scored the ultimate prize—principal of one of the state's largest, most complex primary schools. It was a real feather in her cap, but of course, it would be a wrench moving on from her first principalship. She'd worked hard to create a climate where students saw the benefits of striving for academic excellence, and their wellbeing was well and truly catered for. She'd miss her staff and families and the strong bonds of professionalism and friendship she'd forged. But at the end of the day, she'd beaten a top-quality field of applicants for what she could see was the jewel in the crown, and she was ready to take her skills to the next level.

Kathy met up with her new deputies in the holidays. Jason was quiet, watchful, and a deep thinker. He'd take a while to get to know. Aaron was enthusiastic, a livewire. He left no thought unexpressed and was a bit of an entertainer.

On Kathy's second day in the job, Aaron swept into her office and sprang into a chair. 'Hey, Katie. How's it going so far? Need anything explained?'

'Fine so far, Aaron. There's a lot to catch up with, as you can imagine. But I plan to get together with you and Jason later in the week to work through some things.'

'Great, fine. Whatever you need. We're both really excited to be working with you. It's really great you got the job. I've heard a lot about you; you come with terrific credentials. You've done a few good things in your last school.'

Kathy thought that perhaps Aaron was a little too effusive. And maybe even a bit condescending. She wasn't wrong.

'Anyway Kitty, I feel I need to let you know, I went for the job too. Obviously, I didn't get it, hey, but there are no problems between me and you, you know? The jerk who ran the panel never liked me. I didn't have a chance, even though I've been the one running this place for the last couple of years. Without me, it would have fallen to bits. He knew that, and yet he wouldn't give me the job. Can you believe it? Anyway, my bad luck is your gain. I want you to know there are no hard feelings, and I'll help you to do as good a job as I would have as boss of this place. And in the meantime, I will be applying for other jobs because, as you'd understand, I need to be my own boss sooner rather than later.'

Kathy confirmed that she understood Aaron's situation and assured him she would help him to be able to achieve his aspirations. Aaron flashed his most charming smile, leapt up and bounced out of the office.

Over the ensuing weeks and months, Aaron proved himself to be enthusiastic but difficult and divisive. On many occasions, Kathy had to pull him up and change strategies he put in place without consulting with her. This was especially difficult in executive meetings.

'Right, team, we're going to change the way we run assemblies. From now on, all assemblies will be run by the Year 5–6 team. They do the best job.'

Several members of the executive looked straight at Kathy to gauge her reaction to Aaron's misguided enthusiasm.

'Hang on a minute, Aaron. You, Jason and I need to chat about this before we change anything about assemblies.'

'Right then, what do we need to chat about? We can do that here and now, but it's a no-brainer that the Year 5–6 team needs to run them,' Aaron *responded.*

More nervous looks. Someone coughed. Jason's eyes swivelled from Kathy to Aaron and back again.

'We'll talk about this tomorrow, Aaron, and get back to everyone afterwards. OK, what's next on the agenda?' Kathy took control, and Jason relaxed almost imperceptibly.

After the meeting, Jason called in on Kathy. He filled her in on the real Aaron, hiding his frustration and insecurities behind a facade of humour and enthusiasm. This was the Aaron who had spent a great deal of time and energy white-anting the last boss who, fed up with managing Aaron's behaviour, chose early retirement to escape the situation. She was a thoroughly competent woman but was exhausted from putting out the spot fires that Aaron continually created. Aaron had lots of big ideas but little organisational ability and no experience seeing a plan to fruition. He also had no professional respect for anyone supervising him and could not come to terms with being second fiddle.

'OK,' said Kathy, 'Let's try to make him a better operator. Together, we can teach, coach and ultimately manage him, and he should come out as a better prospect for promotion, or at least a better asset for this place if he never gets a promotion.'

'Reminds me of the old conundrum,' offered Jason. 'What if we train him and he leaves? But what if we don't train him and he stays? I'm up for it, Kathy. I reckon we can do it.'

Kathy and Jason worked on a structured plan, delivered as regular training for Aaron, who initially viewed their collaborative efforts with suspicion but could not find a way around them. Eventually, he found it easier to work with them than against them, and he achieved his dream of being the boss of his own school. When he finally received his promotion three years after Kathy's appointment, he had the skills he needed to do a credible job, and everyone involved in the transformative process was pleased and relieved.

How was Kathy being bullied?

Kathy accepted a job that her new deputy, Aaron, believed he was entitled to. Despite his obvious shortcomings, he found excuses for being overlooked and viewed her as undeserving to be his supervisor. Under the guise of enthusiasm, he put his efforts into ignoring, avoiding and sidelining Kathy's leadership. He made a game of using 'pet' names for her to belittle her authority over him. He attempted to have Kathy doubt her suitability for the job and second guess herself, which had worked when he used this tactic on a less resilient principal. He tried to make it hard for Kathy to confront him or reverse decisions he made on her behalf, including by making sweeping changes in public forums.

Luckily for Kathy, unlike others in similar situations, she only had one miscreant to deal with. Aaron did not have a critical mass of support amongst the school's staff, students or families. However, whenever Kathy made an unpopular but necessary decision, Aaron was able to gain traction with disgruntled staff members, taking the opportunity to stir up issues where none should have existed.

What had the previous principal done wrong?

Prior to Kathy's appointment, the previous principal avoided the courageous conversations that are part of a leader's role. Aaron could have been pulled into line firmly and, at the same time, been afforded targeted support to develop the leadership skills he lacked. Fellow deputy Jason had the attitude and expertise to support the principal in managing his colleague, but his skills were left untapped until Kathy's tenure.

Lessons from Kathy's story

Build a genuine professional relationship with your executive team. As school leaders, we rarely have the opportunity to choose who we work with, so we have to play to people's strengths and work on increasing their capacity when the temptation is to push them away. In Aaron's case, Kathy needs to frame and maintain his boundaries from the outset. Every time he oversteps, he must be pulled up on his transgressions but kept in the fold. As the disappointed would-be school principal learns what you are prepared to accept, they will challenge you less and less over time.

Be as transparent as possible in dealing with the issues and shortcomings of your erstwhile rival. Honesty cannot be manufactured, and they will come to appreciate and abide by your standards (often while working on a transfer or promotion out of the place, which neither they nor you can rely on).

The way forward

Upward bullies do not readily accept formal authority over them. Their resistance to you as their leader goes much deeper than the routine grumblings of human nature that we know occur in every staffroom. The justified bully does not appreciate being challenged to move out of their comfort zone. The entitled bully is self-righteous and highly critical of anyone supervising them. Upward bullies in your school might have traits of either or both types of upward bully. In either case, these people are self-assured, confident and aggressive. Their bullying behaviours cannot be accepted nor ignored.

If you are the principal in a school where staff members feel unreasonably justified or entitled, you are a potential target. Chapter 5 explains why upward bullies will take on anyone tasked with managing them and explores how they attack 'weaker' and 'stronger' leaders.

5

It can happen to anyone

Upward bullies are confident, aggressive, justified and entitled. They thrive on conflict, are hungry for power and have no qualms about who they take on. Every single one of us, as leaders in our schools, are potential targets of upward bullying. We must become agile targets, willing and able to deal expediently with the teacher bullies on our staff. How you position yourself to prepare for their attacks and how you respond to and ultimately manage their aggression will determine their future interactions with you. Your response and management may also influence whether they will eventually give up or move on voluntarily or under direction.

Certain types of leaders are more likely to suffer from upward bullying than others, but the distinctions may not be as clear-cut as they initially appear. Are younger or less experienced leaders more susceptible to upward bullying than long-serving principals? Not necessarily. Do inconsistent and risk-averse leaders leave themselves open to upward bullying? Again, this is not necessarily the case or what it would appear to be at first glance. A victim mentality can be the result of being worn down over time rather than a predisposition to being bullied. Perhaps if leaders were specifically taught to develop emotional intelligence, the teacher bully could be more expediently managed. Certainly, it would be beneficial for leaders and managers to accurately read the emotions of those we oversee, to dispassionately self-reflect and to authoritatively defuse intense interactions initiated by staff misbehaving. But can emotional intelligence actually be taught? And what about maintaining or increasing resilience? The younger target tends to have more energy and enthusiasm to try new strategies, while the older target has more skills and experience to draw upon.

Age vs experience

While it might seem reasonable to expect young or inexperienced leaders to be obvious targets for upward bullies, this is not always the case. Some newer leaders could misinterpret upward bullying as a relatively harmless rite of passage and give it little attention so that the bully does not get the response they were after. If the target is not affected by a bully's behaviour because they don't recognise it as bullying, then, despite the best attempts of the perpetrator, the young or inexperienced leader might not have felt harassed or intimidated. Sometimes, it's generational, and young leaders will not be fazed by behaviours that would upset older managers. A teacher bully who tries to belittle a young principal in an open forum may get a witty rejoinder from their chirpy new boss, which causes the meeting to break into laughter with, rather than against, the principal. An older, more staid principal may be so upset that the bully has disrespected their formal authority in an open forum that they would be incapable of verbal riposte, be visibly upset, and the staff present might shift uncomfortably on their seats, affected by the palpable tension in the room.

Being young or inexperienced does not in itself make you a more obvious target for upward bullies on your staff. However, when anyone, regardless of age, attains a promotional position in a school before they are ready for it, or with the wrong or an incomplete skill set, they are more vulnerable targets than more prepared or skilled leaders. If we, as school leaders, can acknowledge that we are also lifelong learners, we will recognise what ways we need to develop and work on self-improvement.

Unfortunately, some people promoted to leadership positions will never have the skill set necessary to effectively execute their required duties, regardless of age or experience. They will always be exposed to professional and even personal assault by upward bullies. Over time, they are more likely to develop a victim mentality.

The victim mentality

Several traits in some school leaders predispose them to develop a victim mentality. Principals who are by nature or habit more disagreeable, lazy in their attitude to work and more introverted frequently end up on the back foot when dealing with staff members who bully them. Disagreeability means that you will have fewer members of staff who will feel inclined to support you professionally or personally when they see that you are under attack by a bully. If members of staff don't find something tangible to like about their leader, they are unlikely to defend them. Leaders who are slack in their work habits, organisational skills or productivity do not set a good example for their staff and invite resentment and criticism from all sides, not just from their bullies. Leaders who are poor role models will not be respected.

Introverted leaders must ensure they don't always default to their natural inclination to work mainly in quiet solitude. Deliberately isolating yourself on a regular basis will allow an upward bully to cut you off from your school community, who may well misinterpret your introversion as insecurity or even arrogance. If you come across as disagreeable, inadequate or uncommunicative to your staff, students and families, you are likely to become the gift that keeps on giving for upward bullies who cross your path.

Likewise, school leaders who show less emotional stability tend to be the focus of increasingly intense and frequent attacks. If a bully can provoke you to anger, upset or shame, they will succeed in hampering your capacity to think clearly and make considered decisions in dealing with them.

Another major factor in the development of a victim mentality is how leaders cope with change. While we are all challenged by the rate and number of changes we face as educators in the modern world, the leaders more likely to develop a victim mentality are those who do not welcome change and go to no lengths to hide their distaste for it. When an upward bully sees such a chink in a leader's professional armour, they will not hesitate to use it against them. Like it or not, we must embrace change and get on the front foot, leading our schools into the future and disempowering the bullies who would take our schools in a different direction.

Two subgroups of targets emerge from the literature around upward bullying in the workplace—the depressed and the disappointed.

The depressed and the disappointed

It may well be that depression and disappointment are reactions to ongoing bullying rather than existing emotional or mental health conditions. Researchers have drawn no firm conclusions on this data. Over time, leaders assailed by upward bullies may become more risk averse, questioning their own judgement and losing some of the skills that secured them their managerial position, initiating a downward spiral of failure to perform their supervisory role. As such leaders become less confident and less able to manage their situation, they may end up in touch with their own inner bully, exhibit less courageous or inconsistent responses, and ultimately lose their positive leadership traits. It's not a big stretch of the imagination to predict that sooner or later, things will not end well for the depressed or disappointed school leader. Unpopular or difficult leaders, deficient in the requisite skills for leadership and who have fallen prey to upward bullying, are not likely to be adequately supported and are more likely to be subject to removal from the workplace.

If you develop a victim mindset and choose to believe you have no control over things that happen to you, then you will become more vulnerable and will likely suffer more heightened and frequent emotional instability. If a bully can unseat you emotionally so that you increasingly second-guess your interactions with them and others on your staff, they will gain more and more informal power over you. To avoid this sorry situation, school leaders need to consciously develop the ability to connect with their people, work as role models and be highly visual in doing so. While we should see ourselves as potential *targets* of upward bullies, we must not see ourselves as *victims* if we are to deal effectively with their behaviours. Mindset is crucial for success; we must be alert and proactive rather than passive and reactive to avoid falling into the trap of becoming a victim of upward bullies in our schools.

The importance of emotional intelligence

Given that upward bullies tend to be self-assured and confident, it is no surprise that they will attempt to attack anyone in a position of authority over them. While around one-third of those attacked either have or will develop a victim mentality, that still leaves the majority of us who refuse to play the victim. While some may respond to bullying by channelling their own inner bullies, this never ends well. It is preferable to engage and extend our emotional intelligence.

Daniel Goleman has defined emotional intelligence as the ability to identify, assess and control one's own emotions, the emotions of others, and those of groups (*Emotional Intelligence*, 2015). I've also read that emotional intelligence is the ability to work productively with people you really don't like, which comes closer to the nitty gritty reality of leadership and management. We are in it for the long game and need to win the war, not the battle. As leaders, we occasionally have to employ tactics that give long-term results rather than short-term gratification, no matter how tempting that short-term gratification may be. Leaders who display emotional intelligence will be seen to have credibility and integrity across their school community. Their vision for the school will be transparent, and their actions well structured, consistent and measured. The emotionally intelligent leader is not always liked but is typically well respected. Respect across the school community makes it more difficult for an upward bully to gain and maintain momentum against such a principal.

Leaders lacking in emotional intelligence are the teachers most likely to be bullied to a point where they retreat into survival mode and need to be mentored, rescued and sometimes removed from the bullying situation. We don't want that to happen, but it certainly doesn't hurt for us to be mentored, guided and sometimes to accept time out (to reflect on the way forward rather than escape the situation).

It stands to reason that upward bullies gain greater impact over time with targets who demonstrate underdeveloped emotional intelligence, but staff members who bully don't know what type of fight their target will put up until they test them out. After some unsatisfying interactions with an emotionally intelligent target, upward bullies may react by avoiding such strong leaders, quickly giving up on them and targeting someone else or changing their method of bullying from a frontal attack to a more oblique approach. Once they test a target, whether overtly, covertly or obliquely, the bully quickly identifies what will and will not work on them.

Learning to read people—what they say, how they say it and the body language accompanying their words—is an important aspect of practising and expanding our emotional intelligence. We have to be able to listen and reflect, allowing our staff the uninterrupted opportunity to reveal their character and motivations to us. By doing so, we gain skills in defusing and de-escalating conflict situations. And we must do so with an authoritative demeanour. A strong and unbending resolve to call out and act on unprofessional behaviours will build up your 'don't mess with me' persona. Confronted by a member of staff who harbours malicious intent, we cannot ignore it and hope it goes away; instead, we must call it for what it is and challenge it every single time because, as one of my thesis participants put it, 'in the absence of goodwill, you can't be reasonable with unreasonable people'. Or, in the oft-quoted words of Australian Army General David Hurley, 'The standard you walk past is the standard you accept.'

Case Study #5: An unfortunate error of judgement

It was too late when Jill realised she'd made a colossal mistake hiring Tracy, and now she was stuck with her. It was such a crying shame. Jill's tiny two-teacher school had been a beautiful place to teach, a shining example of the cohesiveness of the local people, a true hub of the small and tight-knit fishing community, where not only grandparents but great-grandparents had themselves been educated before heading off to 'big' school in the closest regional city, almost an hour's drive away. The place worked so well because of, rather than despite, its isolation. People had to get along, so they did. It was a picture-perfect village. Eccentricities and foibles were accepted with good grace. There was widespread trust and genuine friendship. It was a little town with a big heart. Then Steve left. He'd been Jill's senior teacher while she took the little ones, an arrangement that suited them well over the years.

It hadn't been easy for Jill to entice a replacement teacher to her little school, and even when she found Tracy, her new teacher was adamant that while she was happy to teach the juniors, she was not interested in taking the older pupils. Jill reluctantly resolved that she would take herself off her beloved junior class, allocate them to Tracy and reconnect with the older kids. Tracy did come with considerable expertise in teaching infants, so Jill was prepared to sacrifice her own preference for the sake of her pupils. After all, it had taken Jill six months to find a permanent replacement for Steve, and a little reshuffle didn't seem like it would do any harm.

Jill had now come to realise her error of judgement in employing Tracy, who she would probably be stuck with until one of them retired. For Jill, that was 15 years away. Tracy was a bit older than Jill, but not by much. Retirement was not just around the corner for her either. Could Jill last that long? If not, what was her plan B for her career? She had expected to stay put for the next 15 years and retire gracefully when ready. She loved her little haven and had no appetite to leave. How could she have been so blind to the real Tracy when she interviewed her for the job?

Tracy looked the part, and she sounded great at the interview. She'd worked in school administration before coming to teaching late in her career. She'd written curriculum, directed the annual school play and acted as assistant principal in a far larger school than this one. Jill and her selection panel were very impressed with Tracy's second and third referees, who broadly hinted that she was rather overqualified for the position of junior teacher in their school. Unfortunately, the panel couldn't contact her first referee, who was overseas on extended leave. But the other two referees were effusive. They indicated that Tracy was an asset and could readily take on responsibilities beyond the role on offer should the opportunity arise. Tracy seemed the perfect replacement for their beloved Steve. The panel was unanimous that Tracy would be perfect for the job.

Tracy was a whirlwind and was enthusiastic and effusive from the get-go. Her energy and drive made Jill smile—at first.

'I know you wouldn't mind. I've rearranged the front office furniture. I think you'll find it much more accessible for everyone now I've moved the desks and phone system around and rolled up those ugly cables that were lying around. And I need you to tell me how to order a new shredder. This one is out of the ark.'

Jill was impressed with Tracy's attention to detail and had to admit the office looked better. She happily handed over the office furniture catalogue.

'Jill, I want to attend our parent meetings, but Wednesday night doesn't suit me. Let's change the day to Tuesday, OK? The parent group prefers Tuesday as well.'

'Jill, I noticed you don't need the video room after lunch on a Thursday, so I've changed our roster so that my kids have it at that time. I've put you in on Monday mornings.'

While everything Tracy changed seemed sensible at face value, Jill began to feel that a bit of consultation and, frankly, respect for her and her position of authority would not go astray. Tracy's assumption that she could do what she pleased whenever she liked was becoming tedious. What had looked like initiative now seemed to be more like downright bossiness.

At the same time, Tracy started making an effort to ingratiate herself with the community and gain favour with Jill's boss, Terry, often at Jill's expense. At parent-teacher evening, Tracy boasted to one of the parents, 'You know, Maree, Jill's a reasonably good teacher, but when I got young Sam into my class, I could see his reading had been neglected. Luckily, it was still early enough for me to fix Jill's mistakes. Don't worry, he'll be fine now he's got me for the next two years.'

When the director visited, Tracy asked for a private meeting with him. 'Terry, I'm hesitant to bring this up, but Jill really isn't giving me much guidance or support. As principal, she should be doing more to help me, but perhaps she doesn't want to help me because she's afraid I'll show her up. Don't get me wrong, I don't want to blow my own trumpet, but I am worried about her attitude towards me and her obvious lack of knowledge about the new curriculum. It's not good for the students.'

And, of course, she quickly cosied up to the teachers federation, asking Simon, the regional union representative, to visit her as 'a matter of urgency' because Jill had directed her to be at school half an hour before and after instruction. And Jill had the hide to say she would review Tracy's lesson plans, observe her lessons and supervise her classroom management processes. Was Jill really allowed to do that? On what grounds could she do that when Tracy was getting better results with the kids than Jill ever had? Tracy shared her view with Simon that Jill was bullying her because it was obvious to the parents, the director and even the kids that Tracy was a far better teacher than Jill.

Tracy's facade was universally vivacious and charming. The kids loved her. The parents, the director and the regional union representative all saw her as a dedicated, hard-working and sincere teacher with what seemed to be genuine concerns about her principal.

Jill had two meetings to prepare for in the morning. One was with Terry and one with Simon. She had not requested either meeting and was looking forward to neither of them.

How was Jill being bullied?

Tracy had free reign in her past school and was determined to take the upper hand in her new job. She quickly made the environment her own, both in relation to physical resources and routines. She positioned herself as a hard-working and enthusiastic teacher, but the warning signs were there from the start, and Jill could see in hindsight that she'd chosen to ignore them. To build herself up, Tracy worked on cutting Jill down. She took to sowing seeds of doubt in parents' minds and put considerable time and energy into extra tuition for her pupils. Her relentless, targeted efforts enabled her to gain credibility with the parents and children and with Jill's Director, Terry, as well, manufacturing a situation in which Jill's competence could be called into question.

Positioning Simon, the regional federation representative, to support her around plausible workplace issues gave Tracy even more leverage in white-anting her principal. Tracy skillfully manoeuvred Jill into a position of reactive rather than proactive management, adroitly placing Jill on the back foot.

What did Jill do wrong?

Jill should have tried to contact Tracy's first referee, her previous principal. While this person may have echoed what the other two said about her, as her worksite supervisor, they could have given vital information that workmates, friends, or worse, two people desperate to say anything to rid themselves of a problem colleague wouldn't have said.

Jill failed to assert her authority over Tracy from the outset. While she recognised Tracy as a strong and forceful personality, she did not take any initiative to set boundaries for Tracy's professional behaviours and interactions.

Lessons from Jill's story

Expect any new member of staff to try you out. It is preferable to be pleasantly, rather than unpleasantly, surprised when your new teachers unfold their personalities and motivations over a period of time. Encourage new staff to be their best selves from the outset by setting boundaries and consistently keeping to them. They can perceive anything else as a sign of weakness they can and will exploit. Remember, it is much easier to mete out increased freedoms and responsibilities over time than try to take control back once a precedent has been set.

It is a mistake to give the benefit of the doubt when someone new does something you are uncomfortable with. Be wary, watchful and reflective—

don't ignore your gut feelings. Either consciously or not, you can expect any member of your staff, new or established, to test out their leaders occasionally. For example, if they arrive a little late and are unchallenged, they may come later each day. They might begin by wearing an unsuitable skirt, then beachwear, and ultimately very comfortable and inappropriate attire.

In Tracy's case, she immediately pushed Jill's boundaries by rearranging the office space, taking control of the physical environment, and effectively taking ownership of the area away from Jill. Such unacceptable behaviours must be called out and reversed from the outset. You don't have to go into a detailed explanation of your decision, in fact, the less detail, the better. However, you do have to be firm and stand your ground so that your potential upward bully knows you are not a pushover and your respective positions are understood.

Develop a close professional relationship with your own supervisor. Terry should have been aware of Jill's misgivings about Tracy long before Tracy got in his ear about Jill. She should not have to defend herself to her long-term boss and would not have had to do so had she kept Terry apprised of the situation. Managing up is an important skill to keep your boss in your corner. Similarly, it does no harm to develop and maintain a respectful relationship with the teachers federation representatives, both in school and regional; normally, they appreciate and respond to you, showing that you value their perspective.

The way forward

No leader is immune from being bullied by a member of staff. It is overly simplistic to label targets of bullying as too young or inexperienced, too soft, or too nervous by nature. Because we are leaders in our schools, we are all potential targets for upward bullying. How you respond to manipulation attempts will determine how the bullying situation will unfold for you. Developing your emotional intelligence will enable you to read and respond to situations in a measured and authoritative manner that will hinder attempts to disempower you.

Upward bullies do not often act in isolation. Chapter 6 explains the role of the mob in bullying the boss and how you can counter their unreasonable assumptions.

6

Mobbing and strength in numbers

Mob behaviour is not rational, it's innate. The groupthink of the human herd has enabled us to survive to become the planet's dominant species. You're not going to turn that sort of behaviour around by using amateur psychology or appealing to any sense of professionalism or even moral decency. Mobbing ramps up uncivil behaviour to the point of sustaining a dysfunctional culture across the entire school community. Once a mob reaches sufficient momentum, it can develop its own directions, independent from the mischief-maker who launched it. It's emotional and volatile and ultimately requires an emotionally intelligent response.

An angry mob (mobs are always angry, aren't they?) is a handy and oft-used tool of the upward bully. Let's explore two ways the mob plays into the hands of an upward bully and examine what types of situations allow mobs to thrive.

How mob behaviour works

Upward bullies who have developed a power relationship over their colleagues are able to manipulate followers by drawing them, sometimes unwittingly or even unwillingly, into the game they have devised.

Some participants will either be too scared to resist involvement or oblivious to what's happening to stand away from the abuse being perpetrated on the target. Unfortunately, people who participate in this mobbing behaviour are, all too often, fully aware of their role, which they undertake enthusiastically, launching with gusto into malicious gossip and mischievous sabotage with destructive intent. Mobbing behaviours originate out of our deep-seated instincts, and they can be our go-to practices when we act unconsciously rather than logically, which is more likely when we're under pressure, distracted or confused. We are social animals, and like other species who exist within a community, we innately defer to the alpha members of our tribes. Bullying behaviours are a routine part of animal society, including pets, birds, livestock, wildlife and even fish. While bullying by an individual will enhance their competitive ability, bullying by a mob within any species is a tool to force a change of behaviour in an individual not conforming to group norms. The physical and emotional cruelty perpetrated by chimpanzees to members of their own community is well documented. Less well known is the propensity for individual chimps to be upstanders rather than bystanders, who will quickly comfort a peer who has fallen victim to the mob. If chimps can become empathetic upstanders, perhaps there's hope for us humans as well.

An adult school bully might raise a mob for three different reasons:

1. When a teacher bully faces a strong and resilient target, they may enlist a mob to help them prevail. If they are not confident enough to stand alone against a school leader with considerable people management skills, the bully will likely recruit followers to their cause.

2. By whipping up an impressive weight of numbers to back them up, the upward bully can take a step back from the front line and orchestrate their malicious game from a safe distance, conserving

their energy and buying themselves valuable planning and reflection time.

3. Ramping up aggression can be a strategy of a successful rather
than thwarted upward bully. The recruitment of mobs of teachers,
middle executives, parents and community members, even students in some cases, by upward bullies, might simply be phase two
of a successful 'get rid of the undeserving leader' campaign.

Upward bullies capable of organising a mob can inflict punishment
on their targeted leader via social and professional exclusion that
cannot be traced back to them. Shunning a leader's need for positive
social interactions or sharing professional knowledge can be a highly
effective tactic to erode the confidence and capability of an erstwhile
proficient workplace manager, concurrently harming and controlling
their unfortunate target.

Perceived threats from outside the group can stimulate a mob to do
the bidding of an upward bully. The teacher bully simply needs to start
rumours to plant seeds of doubt about what the new leader could be up to.
Mob members can then talk themselves into being justified in striking
first before the principal can do harm to them. This fabrication can be as
powerful a stimulant as any actual move by an incoming leader against
them. Their ability to evaluate the principal's actions will be blurred
by the lens of distrust. Mobs that shore up their position against an
anticipated attack can lead to a downward spiral of hostile activity that
may result in a number of negative responses from their target. A school
leader facing a mobbing situation might resort to direct confrontation,
tapping into their own inner bully. At the other end of the scale, they may
respond by crumbling into themselves a little more each day, depressed
and disappointed.

The formation of a mob

Mobs are more readily formed under certain conditions. I touched on one in Case Study #4: Kathy's Dream Job, where a principal is appointed to a leadership position in a new location where the character of the incumbent staff, students, families and wider school culture is entrenched. There may be little regard afforded to the new arrival even before they take up their position. The leader is prejudged, not on their character or abilities, but because they are an outsider coming to 'do unto us'. In such a situation, mobs will easily be convinced to 'stand up for our rights' and attempt to remove a person deemed incapable or unworthy of doing the job that the community has come to expect.A toxic culture of resistance to the new boss can then take hold and cause great difficulty for any incoming leader to change for the better.

A leader who is promoted from classroom teacher to middle management or middle management to a senior executive role in a particular school setting faces different strategies from the mob than a leader who is perceived by detractors to have been 'parachuted' into an executive position. If, on promotion, the new leader tries to fit into their management role by taking on the more supervisory character required of their new position, the line fed to the members of the pack by the upward bully may be that this is the person who used to be our friend and now thinks they're too good for us. The promoted leader who tries to remain on friendly terms with their former colleagues or who is unwilling or unable to take on the required managerial persona can be more easily harmed by the mob. Bullying may take on a more mischievous, even jocular tone, but the promoted leader will be just as frustrated and discouraged in the execution of their leadership role as the one appointed from without.

A life of their own

Mobs also tend to take on a life of their own, building upon the original dispute through gossip, supposition and innuendo so that their target is literally swamped with ever-increasing problems from a growing number of malcontents. Dealing with battles on many fronts is exhausting and unsustainable and is precisely the sort of bombardment the upward bully will be hoping for to wear down their chosen target.

Just as an individual upward bully may misuse the workplace formal grievance system to point the finger of blame at their targeted boss, mob behaviour can involve malicious complaints against the leader of the school community. And, of course, through the sheer weight of numbers, a mob can do much more damage than a bully operating in isolation; their attacks tend to be copious and multidirectional, increasing over time until they gain their desired outcome.

Perfectly reasonable requests by school leaders can be deliberately misrepresented or misconstrued by disgruntled groups of workers. This stance allows the mob to present as victims rather than perpetrators of bullying. Principals are then faced with battling numerous and complex issues, enough to challenge the most resilient manager. Should a principal subjected to resistance push back and continue to insist on upholding the standards being resisted? As site manager, the principal is ultimately responsible for the professional conduct of their staff, but mobbing provokes unreasonable stress and anxiety in the target. Sometimes, it's not enough to know that you are in the right because being in the right and insisting on standards exposes you to unwarranted attacks. What do you do?

Under these circumstances, less confident or risk-averse leaders may become wary of initiating formal performance issues, perhaps ending up wilfully blind to survive their increasingly toxic workforce, as explained in *Wilful Blindness* (Heffernan, 2011). In considering the enforcement of reasonable work expectations on a mob of difficult members of staff, the school principal can be damned if they do and damned if they don't. However, where mob behaviours are allowed to flourish unchallenged, a downward spiral of disrespect and uncivil behaviours will continue until something or someone breaks.

Case Study #6: Are you with us or against us?

'Well, here we go. It's all downhill from here,' Keith sighed dramatically.

'What do you mean, Keith?' Ruth asked. She opened a packet of peanuts to share around, pulled up a chair and took a grateful sip of her well-deserved Friday afternoon wine at the local bar.

The rest of the group drew closer so as not to miss Keith's next remark. He was the unofficial, long-term leader and spokesperson for the middle executive team, and what he said was always worth listening to.

'You know, it's Bill. We've had it now. Sure, he's a lovely bloke outside of school, and he held it together as deputy, but he's going to make a total mess of the principal's job. More work for us, more money and power for dear old Bill.'

'Come on, Keith, that's a bit harsh. How about we give him a chance before you write him off?' Ruth blushed bright red as she uncharacteristically stood up to Keith.

'You're too kind, Ruth. You'll change your tune before long when Bill's leaning on you to do his work for him.'

'He's already asked me to head up a new project,' offered Dan. 'It sounded pretty innovative and interesting for the kids, but I guess he's just after something to make him look good. I hadn't thought of it that way, but I think Bill might be starting to lean on me already. Look out, everyone!'

The group shared a rueful laugh. Keith gave Dan a nod of approval, then fixed the rest of the middle executive team with a serious gaze. 'You lot mark my words. Bill is no longer one of us. He's gone to the dark side, and we're all going to suffer if we don't stand up for ourselves.'

Ruth was on the sideline of the senior girls' netball competition a few weeks later, cheering on her school's team. Next to her, the school's Parents and Friends group president turned to address her.

'Hey Ruth, how are you going with Bill as the new principal? Things changed much?'

'Early days, Beth. He's talking about a few interesting changes, got some ideas that he wants us to think about and work on.'

'Yeah, well, Keith was saying he's a dud, and I'd have to agree. He's not inspiring much confidence in the parent group.'

'Why do you say that?'

'Well, he wants to bring back working bees for the P&F, and he's asked me to investigate a new flashy venue for the formal. We've been holding it at the bowling club forever. No one likes him pushing his opinion; he just doesn't seem to understand how we all feel. Keith reckons he's getting a bit too full of himself since his promotion, and I reckon he's got a point. Dan says Bill's overloading him with extra work to make himself look good. That's not right; he shouldn't be doing that to Dan, they used to be good friends. He'll end up ruining our school the way he's going. Don't you agree?'

Ruth didn't, but she was confused and didn't reply to Beth. She made her excuses and left the game, upset with Beth but more upset with herself that she felt forced to either engage in an unpleasant argument or walk away from the game she was enjoying up to that point. What was happening to her colleagues and the local community? Since Bill's promotion, it seemed that an increasing number of people were rumbling with dissatisfaction, making snide remarks, and increasingly being straight-out rude to Bill's face. Was she missing something here? Had Bill done anything to deserve this, and if he hadn't, what was going on?

Despite intense and ongoing pressure from Keith and his helpers, Ruth resisted all invitations to badmouth her boss. She defended him where she could, especially in public forums, but she found it exhausting to be in conflict with her colleagues at every turn. When Beth made a formal complaint to the director of schools about Bill's 'unfair' suspension of her previously untouchable son, Keith approached Ruth for her signature on a staff petition to get rid of 'our incompetent boss'. She refused to sign, but standing up to Keith made her stomach cramp and her heart race. She took a lot of sick leave over the following months, finding it difficult to concentrate on her job and increasingly difficult to stand up for her boss and eventually for herself.

Predictably, Ruth was eventually ostracised by Keith, the executive team and the wider school community. Ruth guessed, not incorrectly, that as well as denigrating Bill, Keith was now putting considerable effort into tarnishing her character among his mob of eager followers. Colleagues no longer invited Ruth to social functions, and conversations in the staffroom stopped whenever she walked in. Even her students were showing uncharacteristic signs of disrespect. Ruth was shattered. She took to reading the weekly school vacancies newsletter in the hope of relocating to a better place.

How was Ruth being manipulated to join the mob?

The informal power in this school lay with Keith, who was supremely confident in his standing to the point that he expected his views to go unchallenged. He directed the opinions and actions of his peers in his role as a lateral or horizontal bully. Because he was always allowed and even encouraged by his peers to carry on unchecked, he was confident that he could control his executive peers and the wider school community.

To boycott the newly appointed principal, Keith fired off a challenge in an open, normally convivial forum where voicing an alternative viewpoint was uncomfortable. People want to belong and be valued by their peer group. Despite taking a morally correct but socially courageous stand to support the boss, Ruth immediately felt singled out as a turncoat. She knew she'd be punished by Keith and his followers for daring to challenge him. Her stress levels immediately rose. Over time, her emotional and mental health suffered, as well as her ability to operate as an effective leader and middle manager within the school. It is quite probable, given the circumstances, that when Ruth eventually moved from her current job to a new school, she took her worst rather than her best self with her—damaged professionally and personally by Keith and his mob of supporters.

Keith made a likely unsubstantiated claim regarding Bill to gauge whether anyone would break ranks and stand against him. As Ruth did just that, Keith knew who he had to target to keep his followers in line. His motivation would have been to ensure that the balance of power never tipped against him. He immediately went to work on other staff members, the community and even the students to discredit his original target, Bill, and now Ruth as well. He employed a mob to help him to ostracise Ruth and weaken her resolve to stand up against him.

What did Ruth do wrong?

Ruth felt morally confronted by Keith and stood up for her newly appointed boss despite her natural reticence to attract conflict. That's a good thing, but Ruth should not try to stand alone against such an entrenched bully. There are more shades than black and white and more places and people to be amongst than the leader and members of Keith's mob. Deciding to leave is not necessarily wrong, but unless Ruth learned to deal with the bully in her workplace, she would take the problem with her. There is always another potential bully in a different workplace waiting for the opportunity to hurt the vulnerable.

Lessons from Ruth's story

Ideally, Ruth should connect with a couple of trusted colleagues who could support each other and seek to stop Keith from influencing others. In the worst-case scenario, the trusted colleagues might be executive members *of another school. In these circumstances, it is vitally important to have a support group or brains trust, peer colleague or mentor to help refocus your attention on the great things we all do in schools to benefit our students, staff and the wider community. In Ruth's case, getting involved in one of Bill's pushes for change and making it work—despite Keith's sniping—then celebrating its success would be a positive way forward. This would be all the better if it was a project the whole school could benefit from.*

Finding avenues to engage your brain on positive and meaningful aspects of your work will help to minimise the hold the bully and their mob are seeking over you. You can expect that some of the mob will even turn away from the bully if they can be engaged in what you are doing and their work can be celebrated.

Just like we might tell our students to 'find a new group of friends', Ruth needs to take time away from the mob for her own sake. She doesn't have to be the first line of defence. She shouldn't always feel obligated to take the hits for Bill. In this situation, middle managers should, however, initiate professional conversations with your targeted boss sooner rather than later. When the issues are on the table, they can be dealt with. When they are hidden, they will grow and fester to the detriment of all.

The way forward

Mob or herd behaviour is an integral part of human nature. Our survival instinct as social animals is to cleave to the accepted norms of the group. The danger for school leaders is when mob behaviour turns into mobbing behaviour, as when mobs fall under the influence of an upward bully, they gain such momentum that they take on a life of their own. We must be observant of interactions, confident in our ability to turn individuals and groups away from mobbing behaviours and willing to take risks in managing our people to negate the power of the mob in our workplace. We should put thought and effort into peeling away strong, influential staff members and less committed individuals from the mob. To do this, you should identify people who will respond well to things you do for them that demonstrably disprove malicious complaints about you.

In every school, there are seats of formal and informal power. Cultivate the professional support of the grey eminence on your staff, an experienced and wise staff member or a good operator who genuinely cares about their students and the school. This is the person on your team whom others refer and defer to in their professional practices. Develop a strong professional relationship with your behind-the-scenes powerbroker and they will become one of your best allies against the formation of a mob.

Mobbing behaviours are aggressive. People who are part of a mob actively and willingly engage in attempts to unseat a leader they have come to resent. Bystanders are another matter entirely, but their passive contribution can be as devastating to the school leader who is just trying to do their job.

7

The bystander effect

A problem for the targeted school leader is the role that bystanders play instead of the role you think they should be playing. Decent people, disturbed by the activities of an upward bully in their ranks, typically either convince themselves that they can do nothing to alleviate the problem or give tacit approval to the bully through passive acceptance of their actions. They might even convince themselves that the bullying situation is a figment of your or their imagination, to be ignored rather than examined and challenged. They cannot be relied on to support you because they fear getting involved in something they cannot handle. The typical bystander may be traumatised, complicit or both. Speaking up could provoke unwanted attention from the bully, which is enough to silence many.

The traumatised

How can it be that perfectly pleasant, enthusiastic and collaborative staff members go to water when the opportunity presents itself to defend their manager against unreasonable and unprovoked attacks? Why does their moral imperative diminish to the point that their inaction gives tacit approval for the bully to operate? It's got a lot to do with the bystander effect, which has been the subject of numerous psychological experiments since it was first described in *The New York Times* in 1964, as it appeared to relate to the murder of Kitty Genovese. It was reported that up to 38 witnesses did nothing to stop her murder, which took place over 30 minutes, with the attacker leaving her wounded and returning later to kill her. While the extent of the bystander effect on that occasion was later proven to be grossly exaggerated (what we might now refer to as fake news), it has nonetheless been found that bystanders are less inclined to take action when others are present. The more witnesses present, the less likely anyone will take the initiative—responsibility is diffused, and there is moral disengagement. People are less likely to intervene if they perceive that others present are more qualified to do so. They might even comment that 'somebody should do something', not realising the irony of the statement.

With regards to a case of traumatic physical assault where life is on the line, an inactive bystander can at least be assured of living to tell the tale. In a worst-case scenario of bystander intervention, the solitary witness who calls out an act of aggression may pay a grave price for doing so. This was the case for Justine Damond, shot and killed by a policeman in 2017 after calling Minneapolis police to investigate an assault she heard in her street. Mainstream and social media reported this cautionary tale around the world. The lesson for potential upstanders is: don't get involved, and you won't get hurt.

In most workplaces, few people fear for their mortal lives, but the threat of reprisal from a powerful bully is still strong enough to keep them in the shadows, out of harm's way. While such bystanders may justify and explain their lack of involvement to themselves and those around them, they suffer from the toxic workplace environment they refuse to confront and would deny abetting—nothing to see here. From the perspective of the target of upward bullying, it can be absolutely maddening that the bully's co-workers complain bitterly about how the bully behaves but nonetheless give them tacit approval by saying and doing nothing to stop or slow them down.

It is not unreasonable that staff members in positions of less formal power, such as classroom teachers or middle managers, feel that they don't have the strength or authority to stand up to the upward bully who is audacious enough to take on the leader of the entire school. They are also demonstrably negatively impacted by the bully's activities toward their boss. Co-workers who witness upward bullying have reported high stress levels as well as anxiety about being the next target, as explored by Rayner and Hoel's *A summary review of literature relating to workplace bullying* (1997).

Traumatised bystanders may think, 'If the bully is capable of doing that to the boss, what will they do to me if I say something?' When framed that way, you can understand why bystanders do nothing but stand by. Fear is enough to hold the bystander back. They may reason their way out of being part of the solution by convincing themselves that the leader is more than capable of dealing with this bully by themselves without the help of a subordinate staff member. They may reason that the bully isn't that bad, doesn't mean what they are saying and doing, or has an excuse related to their health or upbringing as a free pass to persecute others—excuses roll off the tongue, giving succour to the bystander who simply doesn't have the intestinal fortitude to stand up to a bully.

Alarmingly, some bystanders in the tertiary education sector have intimated a severity of impact from witnessing an episode of upward bullying commensurate with the effects of that event on the target themselves. Just by seeing someone in a position of authority attacked, bystanders themselves were genuinely traumatised (Mayhew et al. 2004).

The complicit

When staff members' emotional, mental, or physical wellbeing is compromised, the spiral of negative behaviour by the bully, bystanders and even the targeted leader is likely to increase. Staff loyalty to senior management and their workplace will likely decline, as will the overall productivity and quality of everyone's output. Where an upward bully maintains a power base in their workforce, bystanders may react with absenteeism, presenteeism (turning up in body but not in mind) and/or quiet quitting (once known as work to rule), which in turn increase demands on a progressively depleted and demoralised workforce as anxiety, depression and conflict escalate. In such a workplace, mistakes are made, and quality is compromised. Blame is apportioned by staff not to the upward bully but to the leaders who *should be running the place properly.* This blaming of the management happens despite the bully's increasingly obvious attack on the school's leadership. Physical, emotional and mental health issues are likely to spread across the entire team because the complicit and the traumatised bystanders do nothing to prevent it.

In Maslow's (1943) hierarchy of needs, the need for love and belonging (sense of connection), as well as that for esteem (status and recognition), is more fundamental to what motivates us than self-actualisation (being the most one can be). Maslow felt that the needs at the lower levels of his hierarchy tend to be the ones that most people make the best progress towards, and for many, self-actualisation is aspirational rather than achievable. Baumeister, R. And Leary, M. (1995) built on Maslow's concept, proposing that isolation or rejection can bring on physical, emotional or mental negative consequences. It would be reasonable to expect that the bystander who craves fulfilment of their need to belong can readily fall into the clutches of the upward bully, who consciously nurtures this need and provides an avenue for status and recognition.

In such a situation, where the more elementary needs are satisfied, self-actualisation in the form of taking morally correct action may fall by the wayside.

From bystander to upstander

Intriguingly, there are a growing number of programs in schools across England, Canada, the USA, Australia and New Zealand that train students to be upstanders rather than bystanders. An upstander is a more active and involved citizen. An upstander takes the moral imperative to overcome the negativity perpetrated by the schoolyard bully effectively. When something is wrong, an upstander will not walk away, ignore, or join in with the bad guys; they act to right the wrong being perpetrated, helping and protecting the student who is the target of the wrongdoing. They create positive change.

Unfortunately, urging tweens and teens to be upstanding against schoolyard bullies seems to be the full extent of current online and face-to-face training programs for the educational workplace. While it is not unreasonable to expect that this type of upskilling would work for members of staff and students, there is little available in the way of targeted professional development on offer to upskill adults in being an upstander against upward bullies in their workplace.

Given that the schoolyard bully does not necessarily grow out of childhood habits on reaching adulthood, it seems logical to assume that teaching adults to be upstanders is a worthwhile exercise for their ongoing health, wellbeing and productivity; continuing the process that has been working so well to improve the resilience of students in our classrooms.

Case Study #7: Reasons to be fearful

'Mark my words; I'm going to get rid of him. He thinks he's just so good, with his expensive clothes, trendy haircut and pretty boy car. He's toast, and I'm going to have him for breakfast. Mind you, I'll probably just chew him up and spit him out.' Anthea grinned widely in Glen's face, way too far into his personal space.

Glen shrank back a little, risking a shaky smile at his head teacher. 'But Anthea, I thought you liked Chris. You told him as much just the other day when he was talking to us about our programming.'

'You've got a lot to learn, Glen. You've got to get these smug types off balance. So long as Chris thinks I'm onside, he won't even realise what's really happening at this school. Chris wants us to change how we do our programming, but he's got no clue how we do things. He's pretending to be an expert, but this isn't even his subject area. I can run rings around him. Now let's have a look at what classes I'm going to allocate to you for next year.'

Glen did not doubt that Anthea was right; she was a clever operator and used to getting her way. If Anthea didn't want to do something, it simply didn't happen. She was so bad that sometimes she even shot herself in the foot just to score points over their boss. Chris had tried numerous times to get her to follow through with agreed decisions, only to have Anthea shrug her shoulders and continue as before.

It was obvious that Chris was frustrated and equally obvious that Anthea's behaviour towards him was abominable. She seemed to take the greatest pleasure in humiliating Chris, either behind his back to anyone who would sit still long enough to listen to her rants or, even more concerningly, sniping at Chris in open forums. On one memorable occasion, the school director was present, and you could feel the whole staff cringe when she started on Chris in front of the director.

Glen and his colleagues talked about Anthea often. Their eyes grew wider with every new shared tale of mutiny and insult they'd heard Anthea hurl at Chris. They were horrified but, at the same time, fascinated by her audacity. They didn't know how Chris coped. Anthea's attacks were frequent and vitriolic. But he supposed that principals must get some sort of training to manage difficult people. It was all part of the managerial job, after all. That's what they get paid the big bucks for, he reckoned.

As for Anthea, well, she was a fixture at the school. You wouldn't get her out with a crowbar. Not only had she been there since it opened and set up the faculty exactly as she wanted, but she was also the most knowledgeable about curriculum. Her expertise was sought state-wide, and she generously gave her time to help anyone who asked her. The kids loved her, and she treated them like her own. Parents clamoured to have their children in her class. Sure, she could be snappy and abrupt, but that was only when people didn't get what she was on about fast enough. She had a quick brain and little time for anyone who could not follow her train of thought. She worked long hours, was always the first member of staff on site and most often the last to leave in the evening. It was her school more than anyone else's, and Glen supposed she was entitled to be respected for all she had done for the place. But she was disrespectful of the boss, no doubt about it. Glen was uneasy, but the last thing he wanted was to get involved. He didn't see how anything he could do would make any difference. Chris was a big boy, and Glen was determined to keep his head down and mind his own business.

How was Glen being bullied?

While Glen was not Anthea's primary target, keeping Glen small was important to Anthea. By scaring people like Glen into passive acceptance of her domineering nature, Anthea ensured that Chris would lack support among the staff. Anthea's brash denigration of Chris' character to Glen had two aims. Firstly, Anthea tested how far she could push his compliance by *saying things about Chris that were increasingly outrageous. When Glen showed no opposition to what Anthea said, she could be assured of his complicity. Secondly, Anthea's open attacks on Chris demonstrated to Glen what could happen to him if he put himself in harm's way. As Anthea had hinted to him, ramifications for Glen could include a very disappointing class allocation. He was also in absolutely no doubt that whatever the rules of professional workplace engagement dictated, these rules were for everyone but Anthea, who blithely shifted the goalposts whenever she felt inclined to do so. Anthea could be certain that as a well-trained and tested bystander, Glen could be relied on to always look the other way.*

What did Glen do wrong?

Glen showed his fear of Anthea through his all-too-obvious body language. Likewise, his insubstantial comments left the way clear for Anthea to boast of her disrespect and defiance of their principal. He offered no contra opinion. He did not engage in any debate. Glen was an easy target, lacking the courage to be an upstander. Anthea would have noticed Glen very early on in their professional relationship, singling him out as someone she could rely on to offer passive acceptance of her bullying behaviours. By showing him her teeth and claws now and then, Anthea effortlessly kept Glen in line as a person who would neither stand up to stop bullying from happening nor support the target of bullying. Glen made excuses for Anthea's appalling behaviours, which enabled him to validate her actions and his lack of backbone.

Lessons from Glen's story

Don't be a target. School yourself in exuding an unflustered, unshockable demeanour, knowing that someone like Anthea will say dreadful things to you to get an impulsive reaction in return. Be ready for the unexpected; practising a cool response to the sorts of things she has typically said in the past can be worthwhile. She will stop saying them in the future if she doesn't get a rise out of you. She won't change how she behaves, but if you don't give her what she wants, she will seek an easier target.

What's the worst thing someone like Anthea can do to you? If it's something like giving you a less-than-ideal timetable for the following year, you can either suck it up and teach more than your share of the difficult stuff or tricky kids—in which case, your reputation won't be harmed, and you'll get to forge relationships with some interesting students—or you can complain, demanding transparency and giving Anthea something else to think about than bullying her boss; making her accountable for her own decisions. The second option is more courageous than the first and may not end well, but the choice is there. When a bully has to battle on numerous fronts, they have been known to pack up their kitbag and find another workplace where they encounter less resistance, but don't hold your breath waiting for this. At the very least, when you become an upstander, you'll feel much better about yourself than if you continue to be the 'innocent bystander'.

The way forward

You cannot rely on bystanders to support you. Bystanders are either traumatised or complicit, sometimes both. Their fear of personal harm will override their willingness to stand up against upward bullies. It is exasperating that bystanders expect that *someone else* should do *something* about bullying in the workplace or passively wait with their eyes screwed shut for it to go away. These teachers have all been trained to prevent bullying of their students, yet they are unable or unwilling to translate strategies against bullies into their professional lives. However, it is not too big a leap to educate staff in upstander behaviours against adult bullies, especially as they have been exposed to both theory and practice concerning their students. The key is transparency and regular training. Call it as you see it. Shining a light for all staff on the fact that you know bullying and bystanding is happening in your school will cause discomfort and a shift in energy. Discomfort and unsettled energy are good, but choose your words and actions carefully in a solution-focused way and quickly follow up this circuit breaker with strategies for change. Staff need to see the way forward into a positive space. They need to know that the solution is available and understand how it can work. Starting with revision around how we move students from bystander to upstander is a simple way to start, then transpose this into the adult context. Use your middle executive and grey eminence to present training so the message doesn't only come from you.

So, there we have the human factors that enable upward bullies to operate. We've examined the nature and motivations of the bully, their target, the mob and bystanders. Chapter 8 will examine the role of environmental factors that contribute to upward bullying in our schools.

8

Toxic workplace culture

A pervading environment of 'this is how we do it here' can entrench how staff behave towards each other and how they treat their bosses, whether those bosses are long-term or newly appointed. As school leaders, we can and should prioritise setting and maintaining a positive workplace culture. However, how our people relate to each other and us is not determined nor controlled by the structures and protocols of formal leadership alone. Place, space and people management are a subset of the factors that can create challenges for school leaders to mitigate.

With regard to place, every school is geographically unique, even from the one that may be just down the road. From urban to remote, monocultural to multicultural, thriving to struggling community, place influences the human culture of the local community and the school within it. As for the space we operate in, worn or hazardous facilities, resources that are not fit for purpose, a lack of funding, or a dearth of capable tradespeople are common problems that negatively influence the physical environment we work in.

Place and space we can generally work our way around. School leaders tend to be adept at making the most of physical circumstances. We adjust our management style to suit the geographical conditions. We repair and upgrade resources as our budgets allow. People management is not so straightforward. We need to pay close attention to how we manage the professional capabilities of our staff in order to promote a positive culture and prevent the rise of the upward bully. If we could just choose our people, rather than have underperformers or subversives thrust upon or bequeathed to us by those referees that only wish to 'throw over the fence' rather than deal with their own 'dead cats', we could make a big dent in the cynical, obstructionist and disinterested human elements that give rise to the onset of upward bullying. But sometimes, those underperformers or subversives are created out of the situation they find themselves in. Turning around a toxic culture in our team may well be the circuit breaker that re-engages jaded staff and prevents upward bullies from emerging in our schools.

Challenges of a toxic culture

It is no surprise that a link exists between a toxic environment in the workplace and the emergence of upward bullying. In such a school, there may be a history of perceived or actual inequitable workloads or favouritism. There may be insufficient resources, inadequate training or unrealistic expectations. There is very likely to be a lack of transparency and effective communication from leadership. Staff may be uncooperative and belligerent towards each other, suspicious of and disloyal towards their leaders and definitely not giving their best to their students. Incubated by a toxic culture, the emergence of an upward bully should not come as a surprise. This bully will have plenty of ammunition to hurl at school leadership, blaming everything wrong on the boss and their leadership team. And to some extent, they are justified. If we tacitly or openly allow a culture of disharmony to exist under our stewardship, we will be held responsible for the behaviours of our staff on our watch. Until we can turn a toxic workplace culture around, we remain easy prey for the upward bully in our school.

The relationship between a toxic culture and the presence of an upward bully is bidirectional; a poor or toxic workplace culture will foster upward bullying behaviours; a newly arrived bully can pull apart a positive culture and make it a poisonous environment to work in. The insertion of an upward bully into a previously harmonious workplace will erode collegiality, collaboration and trust. If an upward bully is merit-selected or appointed to a well-functioning school, they might immediately begin to pick apart all that made it good, confidently setting about destroying the professional standing of their bosses without fear of reprisal. This, you will recall, was the situation in *Case Study #1: Lashing out in all directions*, wherein Susan, an experienced and capable head of English, set about destroying trust and goodwill among the middle management of a previously harmonious school immediately upon her arrival. Think also of *Case Study #5: An unfortunate error of judgement*, wherein Jill employed the enthusiastic and effusive Tracy, whose goal was to overthrow Jill and take her job.

Once a toxic culture is established and a bully well entrenched, it takes a resilient, highly skilled and well-supported leader to turn the situation back around. Therein lies a multifaceted problem for us.

A leader who manages a workplace with poorly established work routines, unclear goals or poor channels of communication is in an extremely vulnerable position for things to get worse. Note that such a leader may not be disorganised or lacking ability in these areas, but they might suffer the knock-on effects of less-than-capable middle managers on their staff. If we allow our school executive team to be deficient in their leadership and management, we, rather than them, bear the consequences. Likewise, directives from above become our issues as site managers, and we end up being responsible for disseminating (too often, translating) departmental policies and ensuring our people comply with them.

Turning around a toxic workplace culture takes determination and perseverance. You need vision, a clear and flexible plan and highly developed organisational skills. You'll also need people you can trust to support you and share the load, both within and outside the school. The work involved in turning around a toxic culture may seem relentless; however, it has to be a priority because inaction on this issue will only make things worse. If we, as school leaders, persist in communicating confusing or demanding work expectations, we face the very real risk of ever-diminishing support from our staff, students and the local community until a tipping point is reached.

At the tipping point, more of the people we manage are against, rather than for, us. Even stakeholders who most fervently want the principal to succeed may question their loyalty and seek more advantageous alliances. Regardless of whether these people actively back the bully as members of a mob, they develop the propensity to become bystanders or participate in middle management squeeze, opening us up to attacks from both above and below. The commitment to change will result in intense interactions and relentless toil for the first 18 months to two years, but the culture should start to shift tangibly within that period.

Dialling down the stress

A stressful work environment has the propensity to wear down a bullied leader. Ongoing difficult interactions with tricky people chip away at our leadership strengths, making us less capable of managing bullying behaviour and increasing our overall fragility. When we are constantly under pressure and worn down, we can default to our worst selves, operating in a reactive, authoritarian or even demoralised way. It's a downward spiral, a slippery slope.

The way forward involves prioritising practice on the part of the leader. It takes an emotionally intelligent manager to identify what exactly is wrong with a worksite accurately, what factors underpin custom and behaviours, and who is currently calling the shots—a puzzle of potentially immense proportion and one not to be tackled alone or in isolation.

It is not uncommon for the performance of a besieged leader to be questioned by their supervisors because they are not doing what they are paid to do, which includes considering planning and clear structures, pre-empting potential conflicts and improving their leadership capacity. The downtrodden manager may become increasingly authoritarian or lackadaisical, avoiding reflection or discussion and lacking goodwill. If browbeaten leaders put their heads down and try to survive, in their unwitting self-destructive behaviour, they cause more stress across their workplace and severely impact outcomes for the students in their care and the staff they are required to lead and manage.

While some workplace stressors can never be completely removed, simple and effective organisational ways of dealing with them should bear positive results. That said, simple does not equate to easy, and it is imperative that however you choose to implement strategies, such as those suggested below, the execution must be authentic and subject to periodic critical analysis for maximum impact.

Communication

I would suggest that the single most concerning issue for staff in schools is a perceived lack of communication, which can be exacerbated by perceptions of a lack of recognition of staff skills, commitment and expertise. Failure to engage regularly with staff, students and the wider school community will enforce those unhelpful perceptions. Members of staff need to know what you're doing and why. It is crucial to their motivation to have a clear and unambiguous understanding of your vision and plans as their leader. Your message must be consistently professional in order to gain and maintain their loyalty and trust. It is much easier said than done; however, a bully will emerge to undermine your authority where there is confusion. It's difficult work, but very much worth the effort for the outcome. Communication with staff cannot only be in the manner that suits you best; it must encompass as many avenues as practicable, be regularly conveyed and always on point. A weekly email to all staff; scheduled visits to staff and classrooms; fortnightly meetings with targeted groups and key individuals; cheerful and enthusiastic attendance at in-school and co-curricular events both within and outside office hours will all assist in building your credibility as an inclusive, approachable leader who knows exactly what you're doing. Keep it in perspective, though, as no school ever gets to the gold standard; lack of communication is always an easy accusation to make regardless of how much communication is offered through however many channels. A reasonable tactic would be to regularly ask staff members if they need to know something they cannot find out through the processes in place, thereby putting the onus back on them to actively participate in continually improving standards.

Valuing our people

Having the right people in the right jobs is crucial to turning around a poor workplace environment. People in positions unsuited to their skill set must be reallocated, upskilled, or, if the situation demands it, put on performance review, no matter how time-consuming, distasteful and unpopular this course of action will no doubt be. You might fill gaps in expertise by seeking new staff members with fresh perspectives to chal-lenge the status quo. People who have been overlooked or frustrated to the point of withdrawing their expertise should be cultivated. Parallel to this, adequate resources must be supplied to support worthy programs and projects. This signals to staff members that you believe the projects they propose are worthy of pursuing and that they have the skills to lead and manage projects within your school. It also sends a powerful message across the community that you believe in distributed leadership and earns you professional supporters whose work will counteract the efforts of those who seek to bring you down.

Like our students, our staff don't care what we know until they know we care. We must not forget to acknowledge effort and achievement, and in doing so, we must be scrupulously fair and equitable in the recognition we offer. We have to ensure we favour neither those we prefer nor those we are determined to win over.Genuine and generous will give the result you need to start to form a champion team.

When staff members feel that they have knowledge of and some influence over issues that concern their work, their positivity towards the workplace and their leadership improves. Recognition, acknowledgement and inclusivity will go a long way to reversing the negative perception by staff and building a workplace where upward bullying has difficulty maintaining traction. In the face of an upward bully in your ranks, these tactics bring staff members into your fold and provide evidence to your supervisors that will effectively contradict claims made by the bully in their efforts to employ middle management squeeze. We make it difficult for an upward bully to attack our competence and professionalism when we routinely treat people decently, honour their knowledge and acknowledge their competence.

A measured approach

Be aware that progress will not be linear. There will be some success and failure along the way, necessitating analysis and recalibration. In the instances where you need to call staff capacity into question, perhaps in a formal investigation of performance or conduct, upward bullies will push back in a concerted attempt to remove attention from their behaviours and place the blame onto the person in charge.

I know I repeat myself, but bullies do not give up without a fight, and they don't fight fairly. Remember, they, unlike most people, thrive on hostility. They do not defer to formal power. You have to be professionally and personally prepared for potentially damaging and debilitating conflict. In committing to the long game, you need to pace yourself according to your resilience, your workload and the support networks you have available to you. Where the cultural norms are typified by a lackadaisical, entitled or resistant approach to the workplace, a supervisor who sets high standards (or even, simply, compliance with the requirements of their department) can come unstuck. Bullies may have such a firmly established powerbase that they are able to punish leaders to the point that the principal or executive trying to turn the culture around becomes a victim of it, defeated, frustrated and sometimes pushed out of the workplace. All four Directors of Educational Leadership whom I interviewed for my master's thesis (Upward Bullying in the Teaching Profession) affirmed that they have, from time to time, personally stepped in to relocate, retrain or even remove previously well-functioning principals who have been weakened and ultimately professionally destroyed by the negative culture and practices in their school.

We must avoid at all costs the genuine and present danger for all of us as school leaders—physical, mental and/or emotional burnout arrived at by taking on too much too quickly, too intensely or for too long without formal and informal support for ourselves. The next chapter will explore the perils of change management and how to avoid such pitfalls. Meanwhile, case study #8 explores how Deputy Principal Carl is learning superior communication skills from his new boss, David.

Case Study #8: Chipping away

Carl continued typing. He knew he had to get the 'Deputy's Daily Dispatches' email out before the end of the day. Staff had begun to rely on it for timely information about student behaviours and welfare, and he did not want to miss a single day, even though it was time-consuming. He'd hit on a tactic to make it easier, keeping the document open all day on his desktop and adding to it as events unfolded, hitting send once he'd neatly summarised everything. Carl prided himself on keeping a balance between succinct and informative.

This afternoon, he also had a 10-minute round booked with Diane, one of the head teachers under his supervision. The boss had brought in this initiative after reading about it in an education magazine, and Carl had to hand it to him, David was spot on with finding ways of getting the information flowing in all directions. Diane would talk to Carl for a few minutes about how her previous week had gone, a few more minutes about her plans for the following week and then move on to any concerns she or her faculty members had. Carl always tried hard not to interrupt or offer solutions. He knew he had to listen, take it in and be considered in any response he made. Occasionally, he made notes so as not to forget points he wanted to return to later. Sometimes, the fortnightly 10-minute rounds required no response. Still, every time he participated in them, he learnt something about what was going on in the school, and the head teacher always left buoyed up by the interchange, knowing they had been listened to and valued. He hoped he was a good role model for the school's head teachers and the office manager, who also held regular 10-minute rounds with their staff. It was a bottom-to-top model, with everyone from the groundsman to the senior executive giving and receiving regular updates to inform the leadership and management of the place.

Carl had time between getting his dispatch done and meeting with Diane to consider the question David had put to him that morning. They had an upcoming temporary vacancy for a head teacher to be filled internally. There were two candidates who were both well-qualified and hungry for the job. One was better organisationally, and the other had superior emotional intelligence. Deciding between these attributes wasn't the issue. Both would need a bit of coaching in different ways, but either of them would handle the role.

Kerry was a player. She was part of the 'in crowd' on staff, the intransigent who fought to maintain the status quo. She wielded informal power and influence, and in her opinion, no one worked harder than her (certainly not the deputy or the principal).

Graham had been overlooked for years by previous administrations, but he kept putting his hand up. He was not a popular member of staff and was offside with the 'in crowd', but he was loyal and reliable.

Carl knew whoever got the job, the other candidate would be devastated. He wondered how David would manage this situation. On the one hand, it would be good to bring Kerry into the fold, increase her understanding of how the executive worked and hopefully give her an appreciation of the depth and breadth of the senior executive roles. On the other hand, Graham's potential, so long overlooked, could be realised. But could Graham weather the fallout from Kerry and her loyal followers if she was the unsuccessful candidate?

The next morning, Carl headed into David's office. Being Friday, David was working on his 'The Week that Was' email to all staff. Just like the daily dispatch from the deputy, staff had quickly become accustomed to this regular roundup of events, achievements and challenges that David had instigated on his appointment to the school just the year before. David generally tried to hit an upbeat tone with a sense of camaraderie, but he didn't shy away from the occasional reminder around expectations, which most staff took in good part, given that David worked hard to build trust. He expressed approval wherever he could.

'How did it go with Yasmin and Rita yesterday?' Carl asked.

'As well as could be expected.'

David had met with Yasmin and Rita the previous day in 'their' staffroom. This staffroom used to house seven staff members, but now all but the two incumbents had either decamped to other staff rooms in the school or not been replaced as student numbers dropped over the years. Yasmin and Rita still had seven desks, five spare chairs, six desktop computers and a cosy coffee table set up just for the two of them. They had made it their little empire where they had avoided and ignored communication from senior executives for years before David's appointment. Their tactics were well known, and Yasmin and Rita were a formidable pair, argumentative, entitled and entrenched.

David bided his time, building up credibility across the staff throughout his first year, until he considered himself ready to take on the pair who 'were never consulted' and 'never informed about anything going on around the school' and blithely went about business as usual, which was of course, out of step with the direction David and the rest of the school were taking. Everyone knew that Yasmin and Rita should be shifted out of this space, but no one had been game to take them on. But David did not give Yasmin and Rita a choice. As site manager, he did not have to. He knew well that as long as each member of staff was afforded their entitlement of space and resources, there could be no reasonable argument.

Yasmin and Rita were not fools. They anticipated that this meeting, held in their space, would be a vehicle for David to try to force them out, and they had their arguments ready. They would not be moved. To their surprise, David did not deliver the news that Yasmin and Rita expected. He simply told them that the entire science faculty would be moving in with them and, going forward, they would be working under the supervision of the science head teacher.

'I guess that surprise went down rather badly?' Carl asked wryly.

'Well, I did catch them both looking around the room at all their gear, doubtless wondering where they could put it all, but there was no argument.

98

Science moves in next term.'

'Of course, you lined this up with the science people first, didn't you? Were there any issues there?' Carl was keen to know.

'Not after I explained as much as they needed to know about the situation. I think by focusing on improving communication and bringing Yasmin and Rita with us, I convinced them that my motives were for the right reasons. It's not good to have people too isolated, stewing in their own juices. Let's see how it unfolds over the next little while. Now, what were your thoughts about the candidates for the head teacher job?'

'Well,' started Carl, settling to the task, 'on the one hand, it might be opportune to show Kerry the bigger picture, but I'm a bit worried she might not take it in. And to be honest, I baulk a bit at what could be seen as rewarding someone for bad behaviour.'

'Yep, I share your concerns around that. What about Graham?'

Carl unpacked his thoughts about Graham's ability to stand up to the mob should Kerry not be chosen.

'Right, there's pluses and minuses either way,' David responded. 'We could divide the time in half and give them both a shorter stint, but let's see what the candidates have to say about that option. Let's get them together, and we can all have a chat about it. Whichever way we decide after that, they'll know we've considered both of their perspectives, and they both had the opportunity to have a say in the matter.'

Carl was intrigued. He would never have thought of that strategy. He was frankly excited to see what Kerry and Graham came up with.

How was bullying entrenched?

David's school had multiple aspects of bullying culture, which he'd started to make inroads on in his first year. Custom and practice bullies had made the most of poorly executed communication from executive staff for many years and had grown accustomed to doing what they pleased without recourse. Pushback on previous attempts to change the culture was easy because staff were never sure about what was happening at senior levels. Related to this was the geographic isolation of key members of staff despite the obvious waste of resources in a room occupied by only two people. A third complexity was that some skilled and talented practitioners had been overlooked because it was easier to give favours and allowances to the squeaky wheels who demanded attention in order to maintain their informal power base across the school.

How did David manage multiple manifestations?

David used his first year to analyse and evaluate what was going on at his new school regarding the staff's skills, experience and mindsets, how resources and workspaces were being utilised, and where communication channels could be improved for optimal transparency. He chose simple things to implement, such as communication improvements that no one was likely to be negative about. Daily dispatches from the deputy and informative emails sent weekly from the principal required only the organisational discipline to ensure they were consistent and appropriately written. Ten-minute rounds run by all members of the executive did require a little extra care to embed, but a recurring reminder in each head teacher's calendar was generally enough to remind them to stick to the plan. It also helped that reporting on 10-minute rounds was a standard item on the executive meeting agenda.

Lessons from David's story

Changing a toxic culture takes time and self-discipline to achieve. You need to adhere to whatever structures and strategies you decide to set up. Of course, they can be tweaked, but if you decide you want to have a regular professional day of learning for your executive staff and you end up postponing or cancelling one or more occurrences or mismatching the agenda to the needs of your people, you won't get traction, and you'll lose credibility. Even in difficult circumstances, such as staff shortages, you should adapt rather than cancel your events. Making a professional day a little shorter or changing the format to online may enable you to go ahead with events despite obstacles. Your determination and commitment will not go unnoticed by your team.

Communication is an acknowledged issue in any people-heavy organisation, and David took care to ensure that Carl was onside, upskilled and pulling his weight. He was also as transparent and regular in communication with his staff as practicable. It is important to listen actively and regularly to your staff and be seen to act on concerns and issues that come to light. In this way, we gain information, insights, credibility and trust. As leaders, we know the results we need, but we can be flexible and accommodating in how we achieve them.

Communication and transparency are integral to your success. To inform, involve and engage staff members about what, why and how you intend to change *their* workplace is time consuming in planning and preparation but should not be overlooked, even in the face of actual or perceived time pressures. Taking the time to analyse and evaluate multiple situations and then knowing when to make your move are attributes of a well-prepared and confident leader.

The way forward

David needs to continue to pace himself, keep note of the gains made and appreciate his successes in negotiating a difficult set of changes. A toxic culture does not develop within a year or two, nor will it be turned around in the short or medium term. However, chipping away at the culture will eventually effect change as more staff tip towards the culture

David is working to build. Every so often, David will have to decide on a 'big rock' to move and will need to be realistic about the effort that will be required, which will take him away from his core business. One 'big rock' at a time is enough. David cannot change the culture by himself or in partnership with his willing deputy, Carl. Ideally, he will bring every member of his executive along with his vision. To do so, he will need to continue to build trust with that group, listening and learning from them as well as affording them deep insights into his motivation and methods. An ideal way of creating this trust in an executive team is to set aside a full day for an extended meeting once per term at which concerns, ideas and strategies are discussed and debated with the goal of systemic improvement across the school. It is vital that David's head teachers and deputy see that they are valued and respected by David at such meetings, and their sense of loyalty and respect for him will develop and strengthen in return.

David took a calm and measured approach to the toxic environment he found himself in. As he progresses his work to build a positive culture, he will need to remain alert to the perils associated with leading his team through changes to their workplace and work practices.

9

The perils of change management

School leaders carry at least three sets of expectations regarding change and managing its implementation. Firstly, there is your own set of expectations and what you believe needs to be done to stay on course. You know where you want to ramp up performance and resources to assist everyone in progressing towards your goals. You have a clear perspective on what needs to be taken out of the mix. You have vision and purpose.

Secondly, there are the expectations across your school community that will not seamlessly dovetail with your own. The expectations of your community will be further segmented into what various and often disparate groups of teachers, students and parents believe to be the best course of action for the school. They will not all be crewing in the same boat, let alone rowing in the same direction. Some of them won't even be on the same lake.

Thirdly, there are the changes imposed on us all from above. In Australia, school processes reflect government policy and powerful interest groups' influence on these policies. Governmental expectations of change can and do come thick and fast in line with the trending mindset of both State and Federal Ministers. Government ministers intent on 'fixing' education on their watch may well be reactive to such measures as poor public perceptions and associated unrealistic expectations of the teaching profession. They rightly or wrongly tend to rely on the results of standardised tests to sanction the need for changing practices in the quest for 'better results'.

With such vast and varied perceptions and inputs of all these inter-ested parties, many of the changes we lead and manage are multifaceted. To add to the complexity, we are constantly managing and leading many changes concurrently. The job of driving effective change in these circumstances is a difficult one that requires close attention and commitment. We need to be mindful that whenever we manage change inexpertly, we create the conditions in which upward bullies gain the upper hand. For example, any newly appointed principal who attempts to rush through changes without preparing the ground is likely to be confronted by bullies and their supporters as an unknown quantity and potentially to be mistrusted or 'not the type of person we want in our school'. Whether newly appointed or established, the principal leading any form of transition will be confronted by change resisters and change saboteurs.

Change resistors

The justified bully will fight tooth and nail to maintain the status quo. When faced with the threat of having to change the way they do their job, this custom and practice bully may invoke the work overload argument; once you start talking about changing practice, these people start talking about workload. They do not want to know about new directions that could potentially modernise or streamline their practice. They make excuses that the way they've always done it is the best way to operate. They ignore the fact that changes can mean working smarter rather than harder. They focus on fostering the mindset throughout the workplace that the boss shouldn't be asking for more when we are doing so much already.

Naturally, when workers feel they are being put upon, the teachers federation (union) will likely weigh in to seek any holes in the argument for change. Proposed changes, as well as the leader who is tasked with their implementation, will be viewed with increasing suspicion. You are likely to experience attacks as a form of defending the existing state of affairs, especially where staff have been poorly prepared for change. They may cite tradition and assumed or actual student, staff and community expectations to justify their opposition to change. In these circumstances, if school leaders seem uninformed or disinterested, our subordinates are likely to feel justified in blaming and punishing us for foisting unwelcome change upon them.

Change saboteurs

The entitled bully will 'white ant' and sabotage innovations they do not control. If they have specialist knowledge or skills, they will ensure that they use these advantages to attempt to dictate the direction of the change process. Bullies who are all over technology have a handy platform on which to outgun the principal, block proposed changes or swing them in a direction they can control. Such skilled bullies can often be found in a position of informal power and influence, such as that of timetable manager, first referred to in Chapter 2 under 'Power play'. The timetable generates the structures of education delivery in secondary schools, and the role of the timetable manager is a key specialist area. The tech-savvy staff member can withhold information about software capacity from a less technologically able manager. If a bully controls some aspect of technology in your school, they must not be allowed to be the sole holder of that knowledge or position. This might not be able to be addressed in the short term as you will need time to upskill yourself to a working knowledge of the technology (through a trusted colleague or a fast-tracked course). You will also need to take the time necessary to identify a suitable replacement to take up that key position while easing the incumbent bully out.

Working out how to get the structures and resources in place with the least possible backlash from the bully, the mob and your resident bystanders will take considered thought and strategic planning. Such a vital task should not be attempted alone. Peer leaders with expertise, your executive team, staff members with transferable skills and your own supervisors can form part of your support crew so that you have enough members of your brains trust to thoroughly explore the problem and a range of potential solutions to choose from.

Imposed change

The influence of an upward bully is likely to gain traction when school leaders are negotiating the way forward through periods of externally driven change management. School leaders are expected to implement such changes expediently to a timeframe not of our choosing. We are also, rightly or wrongly, held accountable for how well external changes are managed and to what extent external targets are achieved. If our staff do not understand the reasons for imposed changes, nor effective ways of implementing them, they will feel unsure or unsupported and will not willingly change their practice. Unless school leaders take a deliberate and measured approach to change, staff tend to blame the boss for the stressors in their workplace. This will not go unnoticed by the upward bullies on our staff. They will take advantage of any sign of discontent to ramp up their activities and find it easier to gather support to delay or halt progress in the face of an irresolute leader. Support for them will be active, in the form of mobbing, and passive, whereby bystanders observe, ignore and therefore tacitly endorse the bully.

Optimal leadership traits for change management

Any leader with a narrow range of managerial attributes will likely struggle in a workplace where changes are proposed, expected or mandated. There are times when a leader who is initiating change needs to be authoritative, even autocratic. Some things must be non-negotiable in order to set boundaries.

Concurrently, the effective leader needs to be willing to invoke elements of democratic decision making as the situation demands. Risk taking is important, too. While laissez-faire management would not be the ideal overarching approach for leadership of a well-functioning, change-ready team, there is much to be said for allowing individuals and teams total control of some aspects of their work. The courage of a leader to step back and leave control in the hands of skilled practitioners can bear exceptional outcomes, both in what is produced and the professional recognition and trust built between management and staff. A good leader doesn't have to be transactional but does have to have the patience to coach. They don't have to be charismatic but do need to be visionary. The type of leader able to manage workplace change, who can manage and settle a potentially toxic environment and negate the white-anting of upward bullies, does not need to adhere to a particular leadership style. In fact, the ability to pivot to the requirements of the task and the times is critical to the achievement of effective change management. Of greatest importance is to exude such leadership traits as a genuine aura of authority, certainly of purpose and a demeanour of credibility.

We need to be willing and able to negotiate in two senses: to carve a path that will see us through the perils of change and to employ superior people management skills to effect genuine change for the better.

When negotiating change within our school community, we should not overlook the capacity of our wider executive team to steward the process effectively. Where leaders introduce change without effective communication from upper management to middle management and subsequently from middle management to classroom teachers, the lack of transparency can inflame upward bullying, and mobbing might gain momentum. Bringing our team with us will allow us to embed change in our workplace. For every change that a regular member of staff needs to make, their leadership team needs to put in the hard yards around understanding, preparation, implementation and review.

The principal or member of the school executive who lacks vision, drive and the capacity to bring others along with us will struggle to embed changes in work practices. Such a leader invites the rise of the angry mob. This is particularly noticeable when a leader presents as flustered or uncertain about the innovations they have been obliged to implement. They lose the trust of their middle management, and those senior staff members may unwittingly assist an upward bully to spread discontent. It is a short step from moaning and whining in the staffroom to passively resisting change (bystanders) or actively making mischief (the mob). Once a tipping point is reached, the health of the organisation is at risk. At that point, it requires superior skill to negotiate our way back on track from a stalled change process. In this case study, Adam prepares well for change mandated by the department, while Zac makes a bad situation much worse.

Case Study #9: Change is coming

Adam's story

Adam glanced at the clock above his door on his way to the first staff meeting of the year. He had allowed plenty of time to set up his presentation. Over the weekend, he'd spent several hours putting together a PowerPoint about the latest raft of changes coming down from head office and was pretty confident it would do the trick.

It'd taken a bit of time for Adam to get his head around the changes, but he'd contacted a couple of members of his principal share network to discuss it. They talked through the ramifications for staff members and what each classroom teacher would need to know to move into the new way of observing and reporting on student literacy and numeracy outcomes. He realised that the changes would mean a fair bit of work in setting up measurement instruments, so he'd already held a meeting with his middle executive and a couple of key players on staff. One or two of them were really rattled, so it was good to talk through how to make sure the classroom teachers weren't overwhelmed by the volume of work they were being asked to do. By the end of the meeting, he was happy that his middle management team members were on board. This was important because no matter how well-prepared he was, he knew he could count on the usual suspects to be objectionable.

Adam had tried to involve Paul and Amy in his pre-meeting discussions, but they were just too busy as usual. Adam resisted the recurrent urge to ask why two regular classroom teachers were always busier than everyone else on campus. But Adam was astute enough to realise that engaging with Paul and Amy would just give them a platform to ratchet up their whingeing, so once again, he let the 'too busy' excuse go unremarked. It was better to concentrate on the movers and shakers and, to some extent, the great undecided than to try to move the unmovable. He remembered his director's advice: 'Adam, there is no point in watering the rocks'. He kept a visual in his mind as he began his presentation.

As Adam explained the changes the department had decreed to monitor student learning better, he noticed Amy making a show of settling herself in the middle of the front row, directly in his line of vision, then firing up her laptop. Adam stopped talking. An uncomfortable silence fell. There was shifting in seats and fidgeting, someone coughed and then Amy looked up to see Adam smiling directly at her.

'You right there, Amy? I just need your full attention for a few minutes. OK, now everyone's ready. Let's go through these important changes.'

Amy got the message and closed her laptop but sent her good friend Paul a meaningful glance. Five minutes into the presentation, Paul saw his chance.

'Adam, these changes won't work. They might be alright in other places with better resources, but they won't work here. We don't have the Wi-Fi coverage to record this stuff when we've got classes. And I certainly don't have time to do that with everything else I've got to get through in the lesson.'

Liz responded, 'That's a good point, Paul. And that was my concern as well. But we're going to get an upgrade next term, and we'll be able to access Wi-Fi everywhere, including the hall. And I've been through the program. I'm going to be training small groups of staff from next week, so we're ready for the changes. You'll be fine with it.'

Paul smiled thinly at Liz. She was his head of department, a well-respected and popular member of staff, and she knew her stuff. Paul couldn't see a way around her enthusiasm in front of the entire staff. He signalled as much to Amy, who he noticed was slowly letting her breath out between clenched teeth.

Zac's story

Zac glanced at the clock on his way out the door to the first staff meeting of the year. Crikey, where did the time go? He'd have to rush to set up his PowerPoint in time. He'd not even had much time to look through it to try to understand it himself, and now he was about to present the departmental changes on literacy and numeracy to his long-suffering staff. He didn't expect a good reception, and really, he supposed, who could blame them? Changes had been coming thick and fast for the last year, and Zac couldn't get his head around them all. The more he thought about them, the more he got headaches and felt sick to the stomach. It was good that the director had sent him the generic PowerPoint that he could simply stand in front of and *read out to his teachers.*

'What's all this new stuff about literacy and numeracy you're presenting today?' Liz asked. 'Are we going to get any new resources or time for professional learning on it?'

'Um ... not sure. Must be. I haven't read all the emails on it yet. I'll let you know.'

Zac kept moving. He knew the staff would be restless if he was late again. As he took up his position at the front of the room, he noticed Paul and Amy with a group of their supporters laughing and checking out each other's screens. He'd be earning his money explaining this complex stuff to that lot. They were a really tough crowd. He had no idea how he could engage them in making this change work; they were always so negative. Taking a deep breath, Zac launched the PowerPoint. He was just three slides in when Paul interrupted him.

'Zac, mate, these changes. They won't work. They might be alright in other places with better resources, but they can't work here. We don't have the Wi-Fi coverage to record this stuff when we've got classes. And I certainly don't have time to do that with everything else I've got to get through in the lesson.'

Amy looked up from her laptop to gauge Zac's reaction. She opened her mouth to speak. But Liz got in first.

'That's a good point, Paul. And that's my concern as well. Zac, we can't possibly do a proper job on this if we don't have the resources to extend the Wi-Fi. We'll need an upgrade before the end of next term. If staff don't get time for proper training so we're ready for the changes, it's going to fall in a heap. And Zac just told me this morning that we've got no idea whether we'll get any of that. That's right, isn't it, Zac?'

Zac smiled thinly at Liz. She was one of his best heads of department, she was a well-respected and popular member of staff, and she knew her stuff. Zac couldn't deny any of what she'd said in front of the entire staff. Everyone in the room noticed that Zac was slowly letting his breath out *between clenched teeth.*

How were Adam and Zac being bullied?

Adam and Zac were targeted by the entrenched bullies on staff, two powerful, long-serving classroom teachers unafraid to take on their principal covertly and overtly. Amy showed her disrespect by openly defying the principal, placing herself in a position of prominence so everyone present could witness her affectation of careless insolence. She made the bullets for her friend Paul to fire, but she held the ultimate power position. Paul hid his taunts behind the facade of a reasonable fellow. His words were not unfriendly, but his confident tone was designed to brook no argument.

What did Zac do wrong?

Where Adam ensured that he was well prepared for what he knew would be a difficult sell, Zac did his best to ignore the problem in the hope that nothing bad would happen. Zac failed to personalise the message for his staff. He considered himself the messenger and took no ownership of the complex changes that would, without doubt, affect how his staff and students approached literacy and numeracy learning. He allowed himself to be overwhelmed by what he had to deliver and how his staff received his message. Unfortunately for Zac, he did not understand that there was not one but two messages that he was delivering that day. The first was the departmental change affecting his school, and the second was his disconnect from the process. He was a leader in name only, lacking credibility and failing to command respect.

Lessons from Zac's story

Take the time you need to understand the changes you are delivering. Consult with peer leaders and key personnel to discuss concepts in depth before bringing them to a full staff forum. Giving issues a good airing amongst colleagues with a variety of viewpoints will enable a greater understanding of the change itself and the strategies needed to ensure it is well implemented. Priming up a number of participants with a 'pre-meeting meeting' means that not all attendees will be going in cold. Those who have more knowledge than others are often ready to provide answers to questions that they themselves have asked earlier.

Expect respect and insist on it when it is not forthcoming. Amy should have been called on her provocative actions at the start of the meeting. You would not let a student get away with that level of disrespect, and likewise, you cannot afford to have any staff member disrespect your position as their leader and manager. When you are challenged, others are watching. Your response to overt bullying will dictate how your people regard you, bringing them towards you or turning them against you.

The way forward

While it's obvious that Zac should have been more prepared, sometimes it is hard to find the time to adequately reframe information to make it more accessible for staff. Some simple techniques to make more time available include telling your administrative staff that you do not wish to be disturbed, closing your door, programming your phone to do not disturb (DND) and closing or muting your email so that you can focus your attention on *that one thing* as required for particular issues but also for a dedicated period of time every day. Make it regular daily practice to be unavailable to interruptions that will disturb your train of thought.

One hour a day should do it, but you need to stick to it and brook no interruptions except for the urgent ones involving police, ambulance or fire brigades.

Giving yourself adequate time to reflect and reframe information for staff should involve gaining buy-in from key players, both members of the leadership team and some of the movers and shakers, perhaps including the federation (union) representative or the residing grey eminence (the informal seat of knowledge and power).

You need to beware of the 'ready, aim, ready, aim' syndrome, whereby you may spend an inordinate amount of time overthinking and repurposing information so that it is done to death and you wear yourself out with effort and worry. Have the confidence to believe that a particular amount of preparation and transparency is enough, go forward with confidence and make adjustments for next time after reflecting. It can be a telling moment if someone asks a question on the fly, as Liz did with Zac. Brushing it aside like Zac did is a lost opportunity to understand your staff's thinking. Taking just a minute or two with Liz to hear and process her concerns would have assisted Zac in giving a better account of both the program and himself.

Zac can redeem himself on this issue and future ones by revisiting it with both the leadership team and the wider staff membership. In doing so, he will need to acknowledge that he hadn't thought the issue through thoroughly at the time of the last meeting, that it was a complex and difficult issue, and that he was inviting comments, questions and ideas around how they could be best prepared for the implementation of the program. People want to belong, and they want to be valued. Admitting you got it wrong (without being too effusive about it) and seeking a reset can often strengthen relationships, trust and commitment, weakening the ability of bullies to find a reason for others to question your leadership. It cannot only be left to ourselves, however, to combat the bullies in our school communities. School leaders must be afforded genuine, consistent and ongoing support at the senior executive level; those above us have to have our back.

10

Prevent, protect, prevail

The strategies detailed in the case studies in the previous chapters should assist you as you consider how best to manage the bullies in your school community. The more practised and skilled you become at managing upward bullies with well-planned and executed strategies, the less they will be able to impact you, your team and the wider school community.

Going forward, remember that the amount of emotional intelligence and resilience needed to effectively combat upward bullies is immense. Schools are complex and challenging enough to run well without the additional burden of dealing with malicious intent from within. To minimise the impact of upward bullying on our schools and us, we need to shore up our defences to prevent their debilitating impact; we have to protect ourselves physically, mentally and emotionally; and ultimately, our goal is to prevail and delight in making a difference in the lives of the students in our care. When we move on from our pivotal leadership role, it is a reasonable expectation that we will depart satisfied and content at the time of our choosing, leaving a distinguished legacy rather than a gap to be filled by the next hapless target. We have to get on the front foot to ensure that we do not fall victim to upward bullying in our workplace.

Towards a 'bully free' zone

As with schoolyard bullying, when a target of adult bullying handles conflict consistently through non-confrontational and transparent means, actively addressing the issue each time it arises, they are effectively positioned to neutralise the attacks aimed at them. In short, if our emotional intelligence is well developed and we have a strong backbone and a handful of grit, we are well situated to prevail over the upward bully.

Once we have confidence in our abilities to deal with upward bullying, we need to turn our attention to supporting our executive team members, who are also natural targets. An interesting side effect of supporting executive members who get bullied is their increased awareness of bullying happening around and above them. Enlightened members of your executive team may well come to you to ask, 'Are you OK?' when they witness bullying behaviours aimed at you. Some may even have the confidence to call it when they catch a bullying staff member in action, whereas previously, they might have walked away or ignored the behaviour. As well as supporting and upskilling our executive staff members, it is helpful that the entire school community understands that just as for schoolyard bullies, our schools do not tolerate adult bullies and bullying the boss is not okay. However, promoting a bully-free work environment while avoiding the perception of singling out staff members who raise legitimate concerns is a balancing act.

The student representative council, the staff health and safety committee and the parents and citizens/friends association are suitable places to start disseminating information and soliciting support for a top-to-tail, bully-free school. Each group would have its own charter for collaborative and respectful communication, and its members should readily understand your rationale. Tackling bullying together could be a team-building exercise for the benefit of the whole school community. Together, you could choose resources to adapt from one or more of the many anti-bullying programs marketed to students for an adult context. This would ensure that introducing a bully-free workplace policy is not viewed as payback for any individual's or group's actions to date but as a considered means of strengthening integrity across the school community.

Safeguarding your sanity

The assumption that preventing workplace bullying is just part of the principal's job is untenable. As the person in charge of an increasingly complex educational facility, we can be falsely persuaded that we must take personal responsibility for everything and be all things to all people. We should not be questioning our own competence or worthiness whenever we 'fail' to achieve what has become unachievable. We must not allow ourselves to be convinced that by virtue of our position, we should be impervious to attack, strong enough to handle anything and everything thrown at us. We are entitled to the same humane consideration that we are rightfully expected to afford to our staff, students and families. We have to take the advice we give to others and treat ourselves with kindness and respect. You may need to take some time out. Do it before you are about to fall over. The mistake we often make is to limp across the line to the next set of school holidays, then promptly hit the wall and slide down it, spending days or weeks in recovery mode rather than enjoying leisure pursuits.

If you've been battling the activities of an upward bully for some time, it wears you down mentally, emotionally and physically. Your immune system can only fight off bugs for so long. When you are run down and close to burnout, the moment you stop, you get sick. The name for this is leisure sickness, and you can avoid it by taking some time off when you need it, not when the school holidays arrive or when you can no longer put one foot in front of the other. We may tell ourselves, 'I can't take time off right now. I've got the (insert important event) next week.' Spoiler alert: there will always be an important event tomorrow or next week. Your health matters more than the important event does. Take time off when you need it, not when you no longer have the choice. If you're getting close to or over the edge, you may like to read the insightful book *Burnout: A Guide to Identifying Burnout and Pathways to Recovery* (Parker et al. 2021).

You need to adopt a proactive approach to ensure you don't spend your waking (and wakeful) hours ruminating on what your bully and their crew have been doing or worrying about what they will do next. If you give yourself a 20-minute slot during the day for planning and reflection around dealing with your upward bully, you can clear your mind for other things during the rest of your day. Those other things should include aspects of your work that bring you satisfaction or pleasure: planning an innovation with creative staff members, spending some time in the classroom with your youngest students, and shooting some hoops at lunchtime with the older kids are all legitimate uses of your time and should not be overlooked.

The signal of an incoming email will take your attention away from what you are trying to focus on every single time. You don't need these interruptions. Turn off the notification sound that signals incoming messages on your computer and try to limit the attention you give to emails; it's good practice to check them twice a day, once in the morning and once mid-afternoon. Don't check them at night as you want a relaxed mind in the evening to get to sleep. Consider not linking your emails to your phone; if someone needs you urgently, they will ring you if their need is urgent.

Aside from regular emails, as a target, you will receive emails from your upward bully and members of their mob. These are likely to include content that details your failings and errors or demand your immediate response to a manufactured situation.A bully may send a rambling rant to you at 4 pm on a Friday afternoon, hoping that ruminating on it will impact your entire weekend. So, apart from taking a rest from electronic imperatives, tuning out from your email out of hours will give you a reprieve from your bully. If you do happen to read a bullying email out of hours, write a response, but don't send it. Firstly, your initial response will likely be reactive, and you may need to refine it later (and you'll definitely want a trusted colleague to proofread your reply before you hit send); and secondly, you don't want to let your bully know that you have been reading and responding to their emails out of hours—that would feed into their sense of power. Send your response at a reasonable and strategic time during work hours. Another tip for crafting your response to a bullying email is to remove the respondent's email address until you are ready to send it. That way, you won't send your draft in error before you're ready. It's also a nice touch to Cc or Bcc your supervisor into the email chain to ensure they are in the loop.

Remember, there is more to your day and, indeed, your life than being a school leader. As hard as it is to put the urgent or essential school-based issues aside, you have to connect on a daily basis with family, friends, pets and community to be the best version of yourself that you can be. Do nice things for yourself regularly. Just as we have meetings each week at school, we need routine sport, exercise, mindfulness, dog walks, coffee meet-ups, camping trips, dinner parties or whatever you enjoy doing so that you don't lose yourself to the negative aspects of your work, especially upward bullies. We cannot allow bullies to bring us down. We must remain well-rounded and grounded so as not to become a pale shadow of our former selves.

Ask for help and expect to receive it

The debilitating effects of bullying behaviour aimed at school leaders must be recognised, acknowledged and managed across our education systems. Greater recognition of upward bullying at senior departmental levels will pave the way for systemic structures that benefit everyone. While many of our supervisors can and do support us on a case-by-case basis, the usefulness of this support is dependent on their skills, expertise and availability.

Until education departments take a systemic approach, dedicating the not inconsiderable amount of time and resources required, good people will continue to suffer, leave the system, be pushed out or take up absenteeism, presenteeism or quiet quitting to a degree that adversely affects themselves and everyone around them. The system will not catch up until the need is blindingly obvious. In the interim, we have to expose upward bullying for what it is and how it affects our work and workplace so that it no longer flies under the radar of those who develop and enforce policy. We all need to establish our professional support networks, which might consist of a trusted supervisor, members of our professional associations or our personal brains trust. Dealing with upward bullying is debilitating, and we need people in our corner to keep us focused and balanced. We have to be fearless and persistent in asking for help and expecting to receive it.

The reluctance of leaders to admit they need help managing upward bullies can have devastating consequences. Going it alone can result in some of us crumbling under pressure and never standing up to the bullies, while others may channel their own inner bully. While asking for support can be seen as an admission of weakness, fending for yourself, including ignoring or going into full-blown conflict, is ill-advised. Both the overwhelmed leader and the leader who hits back may find themselves in considerable difficulties, falling into the traps laid by the upward bully and increasingly losing support from their school community and line managers. In these circumstances, when bullying becomes impossible to ignore, the behaviours will be entrenched and the culture set. When our supervisors are engaged late in the process, even with the best will in the world, it is difficult for them to read the situation accurately and decide the best way to proceed. At this point, our line managers, charged with clearing up the problem, may take the drastic step of moving the embattled school leader on or even out of the system. Help needs to be sought by and provided to school leaders earlier rather than later if you have an upward bully in your midst.

Understandably, in some situations, we would prefer not to lay ourselves bare to our direct supervisors, but by the very nature of them being in that role, we do need to involve them. Developing a strong working relationship with our line manager is crucial to ensuring the strategies we use in managing upward bullies are understood and supported by those above us. We may have to work intensively on our professional relationships with our line managers to build mutual understanding and respect. Complementary to our role in managing those under our supervision, we always need to consider how best to manage up to help our bosses to support us. Managing (or leading) up incorporates developing and cultivating a productive working rapport with our boss, which is desirable in all circumstances but essential when we have upward bullies to deal with.

That said, your immediate supervisor should not be the only grey eminence in your brains trust. Over time, we all need to develop a network of professional friends who can supply timely answers, give informed opinions and fearlessly critique our proposed courses of action. Some of these folks should be at the same level or above your immediate supervisor; they are one or two people you can 'fact check' with before accepting what you are told from above. Sometimes, your supervisor may misinterpret policy and unintentionally drop you in hot water, or they might misunderstand where you're coming from and give advice at cross purposes. The complexities of health and safety, complaints handling and conflict resolution are too intricate for any single individual to grasp and manage. There is no harm in reviewing your line manager's opinions with someone you trust. At the end of the day, the principal is legally responsible for running the school. Our supervisors provide advice and will not be held accountable for the decisions we make.

In your department, there should be some form of professional and ethical standard unit or employee performance and conduct team. If so, make them your professional friends as well. They may have field officers to sit with who'll discuss the ins and outs of your problems. It is best to start seeking their advice early in the piece rather than confronting them with a wad of complex information to wade through. Your department's legal branch is another avenue for timely and accurate information and advice. Call early and call often. The more upward bullying issues the legal branch hears about, the more likely they are to initiate widespread support structures for us.

Other members of your home team might come from your professional collegiate. In New South Wales, we can join either the Primary or Secondary Principals' Councils, whose role includes improving the effectiveness of Principals and providing forums for professional discussion and debate. In providing advice and wellbeing support to Principals, they are invaluable. The NSW (Australia) Secondary Principals' Council (SPC) provides us with a professional officer, contactable 24/7, whose wisdom in workplace conflict has guided many school leaders through and out of troubled waters.

Teachers federations (unions) are another group to keep inside your tent. Regularly meeting with the workplace union representative to chat about emerging issues can help show your willingness to solve problems before they become more significant. It also shows your respect for the federation's role in advocating for workers' conditions, health and safety. Building a rapport with your onsite representative will do you no harm, and if you are a member of the federation, normalised meetings can be a handy vehicle to express any of your concerns or issues. This also reminds your representative that you are also a member of their association, to whom they owe a duty of care. A respectful working relationship with the district federation representative is also desirable. It generally doesn't take a great deal of effort to establish a polite and mutually respectful connection that will stand you in good stead when an upward bully seeks federation support for perceived injustices apparently perpetrated by you.

Tackling upward bullying in the teaching profession

In my opinion, the path to addressing upward bullying in the teaching profession involves a reasonably simple two-pronged approach and would look something like this:

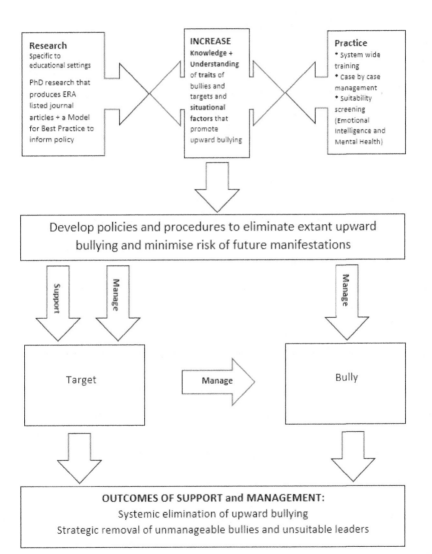

To increase our collective knowledge and understanding of upward bullies, their targets and the situational factors that allow them to thrive, we have to vastly improve our theoretical understanding in order to be able to produce fit-for-purpose, data-driven policies. Sufficient resources would need to be directed towards academic research, resulting in journal articles of the standard that are published in Excellence in Research in Australia (ERA) listed publications (or the equivalent standards authority in the countries referenced). To ensure that future researchers can access the necessary resources, upward bullying in the teaching profession must be recognised and acknowledged at the highest levels as an unacceptable burden on our systems and people.

Along with more research into upward bullying in the teaching profession, we must concurrently improve our practices on the ground. Preservice training and suitability screening both for classroom teacher positions and for executive positions in schools could be routinely applied to our recruitment standards, bringing education departments closer to corporate and non-government staff selection procedures. Regular in-service training driven by newly developed system-wide policies and procedures would ensure that knowledge, understanding and the expectation of adherence to a bully-free workplace are embedded within the system. Based on best practice data, case-by-case management could then be applied consistently and expediently as an early intervention. The ultimate goal would be to minimise the risk of future manifestations with a primary focus on preventative strategies rather than corrective measures. Until we are afforded department-wide policies and procedures to inform our operations, we still have to play the strategic game in eliminating extant bullies—I hope *The Upward Bully* will assist you through these times.

In managing and supporting the targeted leader, we do not leave school leaders at any level to go it alone in dealing with unprofessional behaviours from bullies, mobs and bystanders. The more isolated a leader is allowed to become, the bigger a target they are for the attention of a workplace bully and the more likely they are to move to a reactive rather than responsive approach. Focused supervision and guidance by our line managers, perhaps through regular mentoring, is a simple staff management tool that can prevent upward bullies from gaining traction. The management of the upward bully should not only come from the targeted school leader (though we must show our positional power in challenging the bullies in our workplace). Our authority and ability to manage bullying behaviours effectively will be strengthened by implementing departmental policies and system-wide procedures that are widely known, understood and integrated into our workplace code of conduct.

The ultimate objective in bringing all the above components into play is to eliminate upward bullying across the teaching profession. If we can aspire to stop bullies in the playground, we should also be optimistic about our ability to extend this to our adult population. Where bullies are unmanageable, we should be able to move them out of the system, and emergent policy should make that an avenue available to us should the situation warrant it. Where school leaders have been irretrievably damaged by an upward bully, policy should afford them a way out with dignity and respect.

Final thoughts

The disempowering impact of upward bullying can stop a school in its tracks so that leadership is not about the kids anymore but about fixing a broken establishment. As well as destroying the culture of a school and disabling the education outcomes for the student body, the behaviour of upward bullies may result in severe health issues for their target, that person's family and friends, the wider school community and even the physical and mental health of the bully themselves. There are no winners where upward bullying is allowed to manifest and grow.

Upward bullies, contrary to popular belief, do not pick easy targets. Their targets are whoever has formal power over them. They will attack both strong and weak leaders. The leader's reaction under attack will determine the path the bully takes. With a more susceptible leader, the bully will use a direct one-on-one approach. When the leader is resistant, the bully will switch to mobilising a mob and more oblique tactics that can leave the leader questioning their own motivations and abilities.

It should not be up to individual school leaders to bear the burden of the bully in their school. System-wide recognition and acknowledgement of the impact of upward bullying lag behind an obvious and urgent need, so we must proactively seek support when confronted with upward bullying. Thankfully, structures and systems are changing, and targets of upward bullying who ask for help might receive it. However, there are clear gaps that senior departmental executives, workplace health and safety officials, employee performance and conduct units and our teachers federations (unions) could explore in consultation with school executive staff to move to a more proactive approach for early identification and intervention. There is a need to focus on cultivating school leadership capacity, including developing the interpersonal skills of targeted leaders who respond to upward bullying in imprudent ways. It is optimal that school leaders, present and future, have highly developed emotional intelligence and superior resilience. Ideally, we require the capacity to recognise bullying behaviour and formulate a system-wide policy for its management.

Upward bullies must not be allowed to disrupt the core business of our schools, disempower our leaders and managers and spoil the educational experiences of our students. If you have an upward bully in your school community, you need to read the situation, take a measured and considered response, take care of yourself and build your support network around you. I encourage you to lobby for systemic change and, in the meantime, when you hit on a structure or strategy that works for you, pay or send it forward far and wide to help free our schools from upward bullying.

References

Preface

Riley, P., See, S-M., Marsh, H., & Dicke, T. (2021) 'The Australian Principal Occupational Health, Safety and Wellbeing Survey (IPPE Report)'. Institute for Positive Psychology and Education, Australian Catholic University. Retrieved from www.healthandwellbeing.org/reports/AU/2021_ACU_Principals_HWB_Final_Report.pdf

Chapter 1

Rosner, S. 'Upward Bullying in the Workplace: a literature review'. The Upward Bully. Retrieved from theupwardbully.com/research

Australian Principal Occupational Health, Safety and Wellbeing Survey website: www.principalhealth.org/reports.php

Chapter 2

Branch, S., Sheehan, M., Barker, M., & Ramsay, S. (2004). 'Perceptions of Upwards Bullying: An Interview Study'. Paper presented at the 4th International Conference on Bullying and Harassment in the Workplace. Retrieved from www.researchgate.net/publication/29460127_Perceptions_of_Upwards_Bullying_An_Interview_Study

Einarsen, S. (2000). 'Harassment and bullying at work: A review of the Scandinavian approach'. *Aggression and Violent Behavior*, 5(4), 379–401. Retrieved from doi.org/10.1016/S1359-1789(98)00043-3

Hadikin, R., & O'Driscoll, M. (2000). *The Bullying Culture: Cause, Effect, Harm reduction*. Books for Midwives. Press: Oxford. Health and Safety Executive. (1995)

Rayner, C., Hoel, H., & Cooper, C. (2001). *Workplace Bullying: What we know, who is to blame and what can we do?* CRC Press.

Chapter 3

Rosner, S. 'Upward Bullying in the Workplace: a literature review'. The Upward Bully. Retrieved from theupwardbully.com/research

Riley, D. E., Duncan, D. J., & Edwards, J. (2012). *Bullying of Staff in Schools*. ACER Press.

Namie, G., Namie, R. (2007) U.S. Workplace Bullying Survey: September, 2007. Waitt Institute for Violence Prevention. Retrieved from https://workplacebullying.org/multi/pdf/WBIsurvey2007.pdf

Mintz-Binder, R. D., & Calkins, R. D. (2012). 'Exposure to bullying at the associate degree nursing program director level'. *Teaching and Learning in Nursing*, 7(4), 152–158.

Branch, S., Sheehan, M., Barker, M., & Ramsay, S. (2004). 'Perceptions of upwards bullying: An interview study'. Paper presented at the 4th International Conference on Bullying and Harassment in the Workplace.

Lee, F. (1997). 'When the going gets tough, do the tough ask for help? Help seeking and power motivation in organizations'. *Organizational Behavior and Human Decision Processes*, 72(3), 336–363.

Ariza-Montes, J. A., Muniz R, N. M., Leal-Rodríguez, A. L., & Leal-Millán, A. G. (2014). 'Workplace Bullying among Managers: A Multifactorial perspective and understanding'. *International Journal of Environmental Research and Public Health*, 11(3), 2657–2682.

Andersson, L. M., & Pearson, C. M. (1999). 'Tit for Tat? The Spiralling Effect of Incivility in the Workplace'. *Academy of Management Review*, 24(3), 452–471.

Philip Riley's longitudinal principal wellbeing surveys available at www.principalhealth.org.

Chapter 4

Twenge, J. M., & Campbell, W. K. (2009). The Narcissism Epidemic: Living in the Age of Entitlement. Simon and Schuster.

Branch, S., Sheehan, M., Barker, M., & Ramsay, S. (2004). Perceptions of upwards bullying: An interview study. Paper presented at the 4th International Conference on Bullying and Harassment in the Workplace.

Chapter 5

Goleman, D. (1996). *Emotional Intelligence: Why it can matter more than IQ*. Bloomsbury Publishing.

Chapter 6

Heffernan, M. (2011). *Wilful Blindness: Why We Ignore the Obvious*. Simon and Schuster.

Chapter 7

Rayner, C., & Hoel, H. (1997). 'A summary review of literature relating to workplace bullying'. *Journal of Community & Applied Social Psychology*, 7(3), 181–191.

Mayhew, C., McCarthy, P., Chappell, D., Quinlan, M., Barker, M., & Sheehan, M. (2004). 'Measuring the extent of impact from occupational violence and bullying on traumatised workers'. *Employee Responsibilities and Rights Journal*, 16(3), 117–134.

Cherry, K. (2022). 'Maslow's Hierarchy of Needs'. Verywellmind. Retrieved from www.verywellmind.com/what-is-maslows-hierarchy-of-needs-4136760

Baumeister, R. F., & Leary, M. R. (1995). 'The need to belong: Desire for interpersonal attachments as a fundamental human motivation'. *Interpersonal Development*, 57–89.

Chapter 8

Rosner, S. (2018). 'Upward bullying in education; what the research is telling us'. *Education Today*, 31, 30–33.

Rosner, S. (2019). 'Upward bullying in education; the current situation'. *Education Today*, 32, 40–42

James, T. (2018). 'The power of 10 Minutes – developing a trusting relationship with school leaders', *Education Today*. Retrieved from www.educationtoday.com.au/_images/articles/pdf/article-pdf-1467.pdf

Chapter 10

Parker, G., Tavella, G., & Eyers, K. (2021). *Burnout: A Guide to Identifying Burnout and Pathways to Recovery.* Allen & Unwin.

Printed in Great Britain
by Amazon

43243005R00089